THE BEST OF
BUSINESS 7
CARD
DESIGN
LOEWY: LONDON

ROCKPORT

© 2006 BY ROCKPORT
PUBLISHERS, INC.

10 9 8 7 6 5 4 3 2 1

FIRST PUBLISHED IN THE UNITED STATES OF AMERICA BY
ROCKPORT PUBLISHERS, A MEMBER OF
QUAYSIDE PUBLISHING GROUP
33 COMMERCIAL STREET
GLOUCESTER,
MASSACHUSETTS 01930-5089
TELEPHONE: (978) 282-9590
FAX: (978) 283-2742
WWW.ROCKPUB.COM

DESIGN: LOEWY
COVER IMAGE: LOEWY

PRINTED IN CHINA

ISBN 1-59253-220-9

TYLER BLIK, Principal
655 G STREET, SUITE E SAN DIEGO, CA 92101 PH. 619.234.4434 FX. 619.234.4494
tyler@tylerblik.com WWW.TYLERBLIK.COM

IDEAS THAT MAKE

FOOD
FOR THOUGHT

Events catered for
from £3.50 per person

HOW'S
GYM
GOING?

Salads from £2.95

NGS HAPPEN.

THE BEST OF
BUSINESS
CARD
DESIGN

LOEWY: LONDON

7

INTRODUCTION

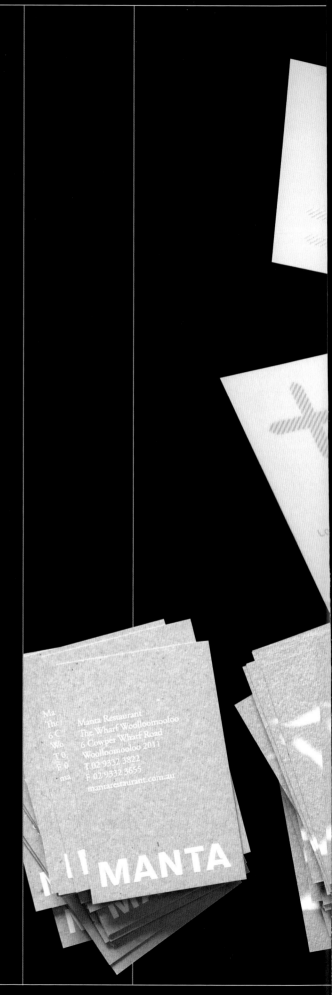

YOUR BUSINESS CARD IS A STATEMENT WHICH SPEAKS VOLUMES ABOUT YOU—AND YOUR ORGANIZATION. A BUSINESS CARD SHOULD BE AN OBJECT OF PRIDE. IT SHOULD CONVEY A PERSONALITY, AND BE SOMETHING YOU'RE PROUD TO HAND OVER. AFTER ALL, PEOPLE DON'T BUY A COMPANY THESE DAYS—THEY BUY ITS PEOPLE. WE'VE READ A HUNDRED TIMES THAT A BUSINESS CARD IS A GREAT WAY OF MAKING A GOOD FIRST IMPRESSION. AND YET EXPERIENCE HAS TAUGHT US THAT, IN REALITY, THEY OFTEN SAY VERY LITTLE ABOUT WHO WE ARE.

IN JAPAN THE EXCHANGE OF CARDS IS A FORMAL OCCASION; IT'S A RITUAL THAT IS STEEPED IN HONOR AND TRADITION. INDIVIDUALS GREET AND BOW HEADS, THEN THE CARDS ARE EXCHANGED AND THE DETAILS STUDIED. THE NAMES ARE READ ALOUD IN TURN, ENSURING CORRECT PRONUNCIATION. IT'S A BUSINESS TRANSACTION, YET IT'S IMBUED WITH A SENSE OF PERSONAL RESPECT FOR EVERYONE INVOLVED.

THIS BOOK IS A CELEBRATION OF BOLD STATEMENTS. AS SUCH, IT RECOGNIZES AND APPRECIATES THE CONFIDENCE TO SAY "THIS IS WHO WE ARE." THE RANGE OF CARDS FEATURED IS SOMEWHAT ALL ENCOMPASSING —FROM FUN TO SERIOUS, MINIMAL TO MAXIMAL—BUT THERE IS A COMMON THREAD THROUGHOUT: EACH AND EVERY CARD HAS A PERSONALITY. EACH AND EVERY ONE HAS BEEN DESIGNED WITH PRIDE, AND THAT CAN ONLY COMMAND RESPECT.

PAUL BURGESS LOEWY

CREATIVE DIRECTOR
PAUL BURGESS

ART DIRECTOR
BEN WOOD

JUDGES
PAUL BURGESS
BEN WOOD
GRAHAM FARR
CHRISTINA MADSEN
RYAN MILLER
BEN EDWARDS

ARTWORKER
PETE USHER

indulge restaurant bar
184 burgundy street
heidelberg 3084 victoria
telephone 03 9458 2222
facsimile 03 9458 5164

001
OCTAVO
AUSTRALIA
ART DIRECTOR
GARY DOMONEY
CLIENT
INDULGE RESTAURANT BAR
PAPER/MATERIALS
360 GSM WHITE A ARTBOARD

002
KEARNEYROCHOLL
GERMANY
ART DIRECTOR
FRANK ROCHOLL
DESIGNER
SVEN KILS
CLIENT
AXON KITCHENWORKS GMBH
PAPER/MATERIALS
CHROMOLUX METALLIC DARK GREY

AXON
KITCHEN WORKS

www.axon-kitchenworks.com

suzy jurist
president

sji associates, inc.
design & advertisi

1001 sixth avenu
new york, n
t 212. 391
f 212.
sjiasso
suzy@sji

003
SJI ASSOCIATES
USA
ART DIRECTOR
JILL VINITSKY
DESIGNERS
KAREN LEMCKE
GT GOTO
CLIENT
SJI ASSOCIATES
PAPER/MATERIALS
SMART PAPERS
BENEFIT
SKINNY LATTÉ

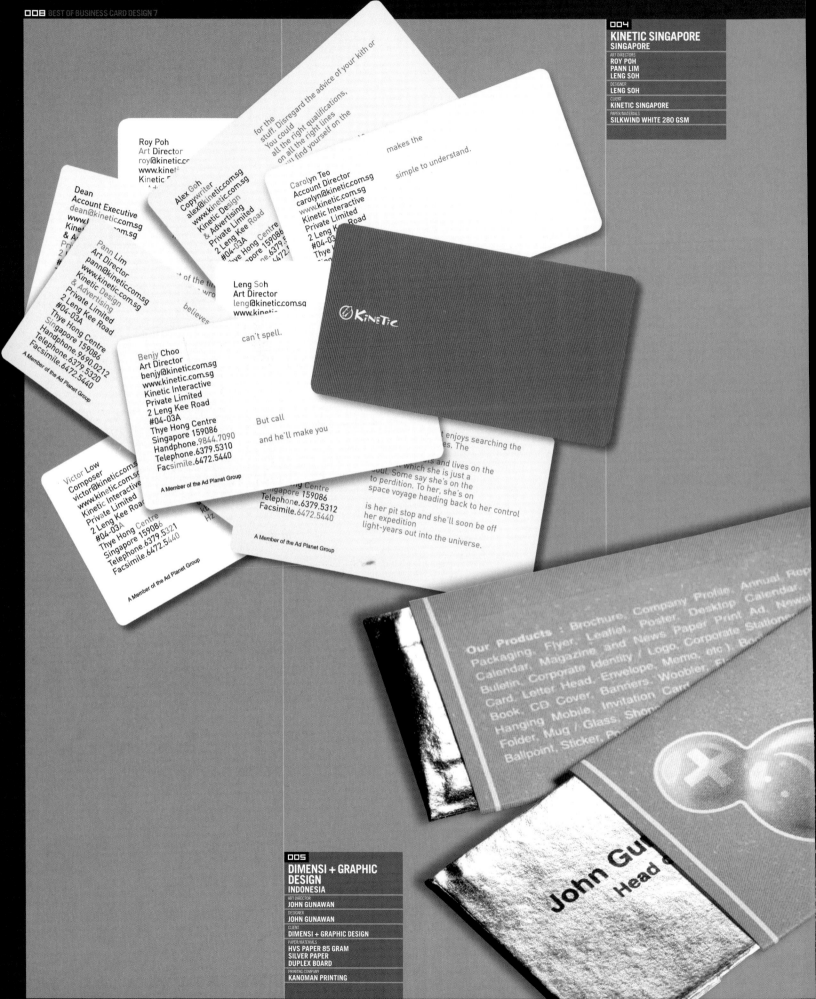

Roy Poh
Art Director
roy@kinetic.
www.kineti
Kinetic

Dean
Account Executive
dean@k
Kineti
.com.sg
& A
Pri

Alex Goh
Copywriter
alex@kinetic.com.sg
www.kinetic.com.sg
Kinetic Design
& Advertising
Private Limited
2 Leng Kee Road
#04-03A
Thye Hong Centre
apore 159086
6379.5

for the
stuff. Disregard the advice of your kith or
You could
all the right qualifications,
on all the right lines
ill find yourself on the

makes the

simple to understand.

Carolyn Teo
Account Director
carolyn@kinetic.com.sg
www.kinetic.com.sg
Kinetic Interactive
Private Limited
2 Leng Kee Road
#04-03
Thye

Pann Lim
Art Director
pann@kinetic.com.sg
Kinetic Design
& Advertising
Private Limited
2 Leng Kee Road
#04-03A
Thye Hong Centre
Singapore 159086
Handphone.9690.0212
Telephone.6379.5320
Facsimile.6472.5440
A Member of the Ad Planet Group

Leng Soh
Art Director
leng@kinetic.com.sg
www.kineti

can't spell.

Benjy Choo
Art Director
benjy@kinetic.com.sg
www.kinetic.com.sg
Kinetic Interactive
Private Limited
2 Leng Kee Road
#04-03A
Thye Hong Centre
Singapore 159086
Handphone.9844.7090
Telephone.6379.5310
Facsimile.6472.5440
A Member of the Ad Planet Group

But call

and he'll make you

Victor Low
Composer
victor@kinetic.com.s
www.kinetic.com.s
Kinetic Interactive
Private Limited
2 Leng Kee Road
#04-03A
Thye Hong Centre
Singapore.6379.5321
Telephone.6472.5440
Facsimile.6472.5440
A Member of the Ad Planet Group

Hz

g Centre
Singapore 159086
Telephone.6379.5312
Facsimile.6472.5440

A Member of the Ad Planet Group

enjoys searching the
es. The

s and lives on the
which she is just a
oul. Some say she's on the
to perdition. To her, she's on
space voyage heading back to her control

is her pit stop and she'll soon be off
her expedition
light-years out into the universe.

⊘KiNeTiC

Our Products : Brochure, Company Profile, Annual, Rep
Packaging, Flyer, Leaflet, Poster, Desktop Calendar,
Calendar, Magazine and News Paper Print Ad, News
Buletin, Corporate Identity / Logo, Corporate Stationer
Card, Letter Head, Envelope, Memo, etc.), Bo
Book, CD Cover, Banners, Woobler, F
Hanging Mobile, Invitation Card
Folder, Mug / Glass, Shor
Ballpoint, Sticker, Po

John Gu
Head o

004

KINETIC SINGAPORE
SINGAPORE

ART DIRECTORS
**ROY POH
PANN LIM
LENG SOH**

DESIGNER
LENG SOH

CLIENT
KINETIC SINGAPORE

PAPER/MATERIALS
SILKWIND WHITE 280 GSM

005

DIMENSI + GRAPHIC
DESIGN
INDONESIA

ART DIRECTOR
JOHN GUNAWAN

DESIGNER
JOHN GUNAWAN

CLIENT
DIMENSI + GRAPHIC DESIGN

PAPER/MATERIALS
**HVS PAPER 85 GRAM
SILVER PAPER
DUPLEX BOARD**

PRINTING COMPANY
KANOMAN PRINTING

Q
Sonnenberger Straße 16
65193 Wiesbaden

T (06 11) 18 13 10
F (06 11) 18 13 118

tvd@q-home.de
www.q-home.de

Q

Thilo von Debschitz
Geschäftsführer

KONZEPTION, DESIGN UND REALISATION FÜR PRINT UND NEUE MEDIEN

007
Q
GERMANY
ART DIRECTOR
THILO VON DEBSCHITZ
DESIGNER
MARCEL KUMMERER
CLIENT
Q

DIMENSI+
GRAPHIC DESIGN
EXCELLENT TASTE

006
ZION GRAPHICS
SWEDEN
ART DIRECTOR
RICKY TILLBLAD
DESIGNER
RICKY TILLBLAD
CLIENT
SIZE RECORDS

● COMPANY
SIZE RECORDS
● NAME   ● TITLE
STEVE ANGELLO LABEL MANAGER / PRODUCER
● ADDRESS
TUNVÄGEN 24. SE-170 68 SOLNA. STOCKHOLM
● PHONE   ● MOBILE
+46 8 624 04 03 +46 8 704 55 54 59
● E-MAIL
STEVE@SIZERECORDS.COM WWW.SIZERECORDS.COM

008
JIM O'CONNOR
COPYWRITING
UNITED KINGDOM
ART DIRECTOR
JIM O'CONNOR
DESIGNER
JIM O'CONNOR
CLIENT
JIM O'CONNOR
PAPER/MATERIALS
CARD

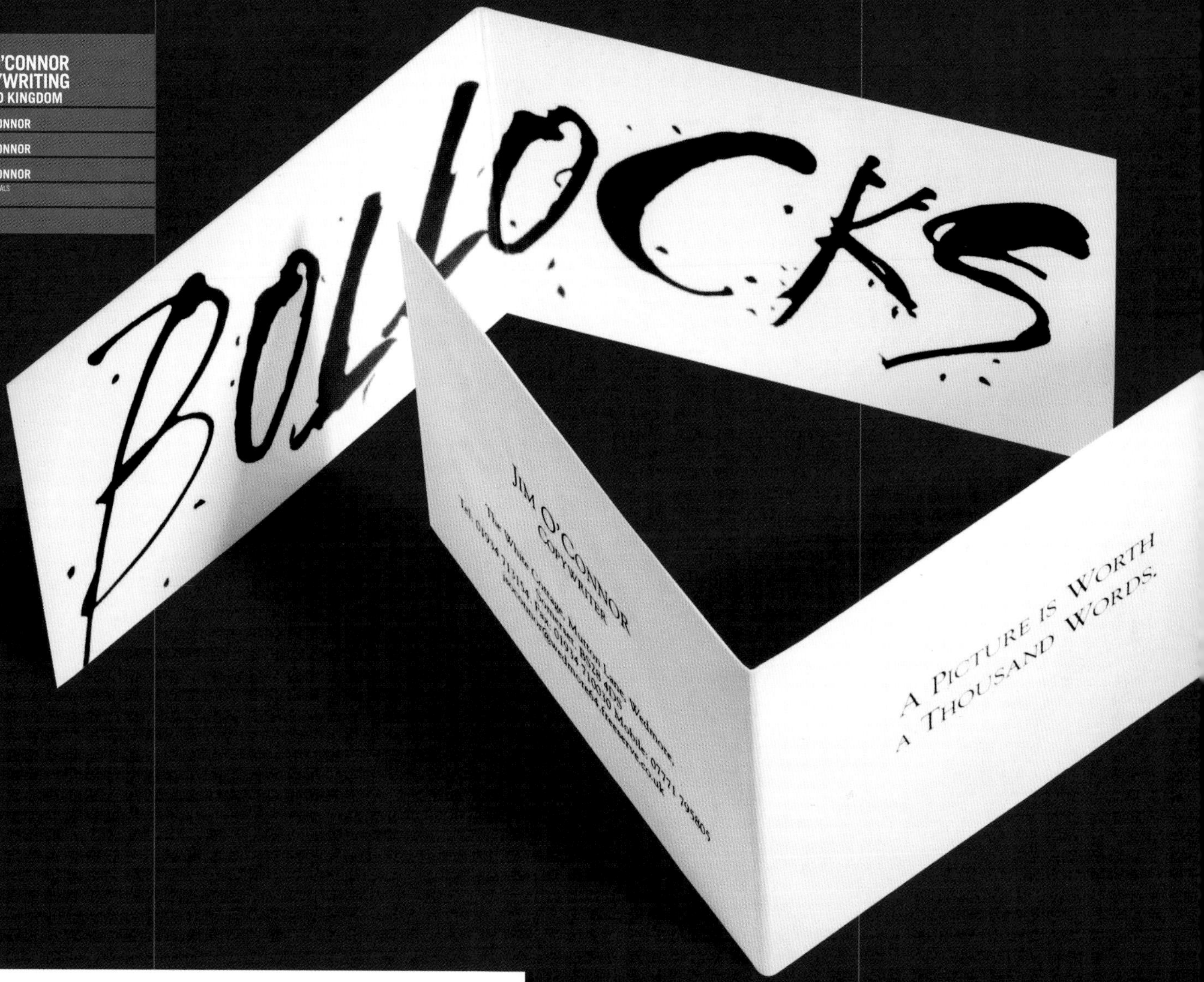

BOLLOCKS

JIM O'CONNOR
COPYWRITER

A PICTURE IS WORTH
A THOUSAND WORDS.

fox

Theresa Allegretta

2 Oliver Street
» Boston MA 02109
» www.foxcorp.com

e » tallegretta@foxcorp.com
t » 617.946.2429
f » 617.946.2414

FOX Relocation Management Corp.
Boston New York Washington Providence

009
SELTZER DESIGN
USA
ART DIRECTOR
ROCHELLE SELTZER
DESIGNER
ANNIE SMIDT
CLIENT
FOX

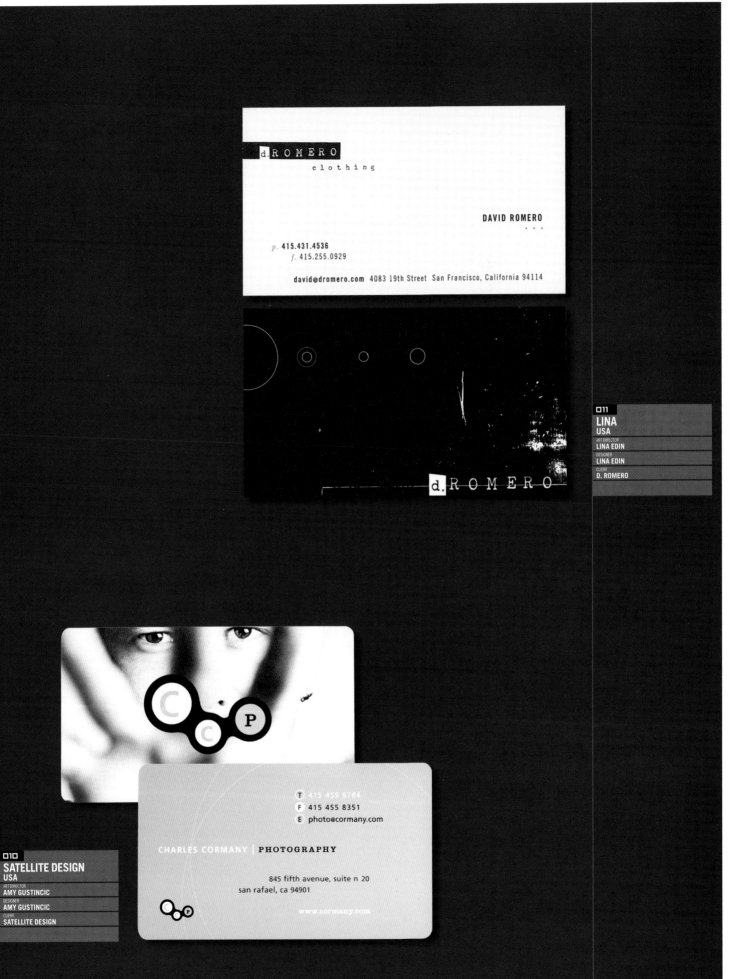

□11
LINA
USA
ART DIRECTOR
LINA EDIN
DESIGNER
LINA EDIN
CLIENT
D. ROMERO

□10
SATELLITE DESIGN
USA
ART DIRECTOR
AMY GUSTINCIC
DESIGNER
AMY GUSTINCIC
CLIENT
SATELLITE DESIGN

Horizon Design Retail Design & Strategy

London Paris Frankfurt Madrid

Waverley House Lower Square
Isleworth London England TW7 6RL
T: +44 [0] 181 560 9393 F: +44 [0] 181 568 6900
E: info@horizondesign.co.uk W: www.horizondesign.co.uk

Gareth Thomas Design Director

012
NB:STUDIO
UNITED KINGDOM
ART DIRECTORS
NICK FINNEY
BEN STOTT
CLIENT
HORIZON

013
FUNNEL
USA
DESIGNER
ERIC KASS
CLIENT
ELLEN JACKSON PORTRAITURE
PAPER/MATERIALS
REALLY THICK BOARD

INDIANAPOLIS, IND

Memories preserved.
Fine prints can be had at any time

Ellen Jackson

PORTRAITURE

ELLENJACKSONPORTRAITS.COM

AREA CODE

:317:

590/5071

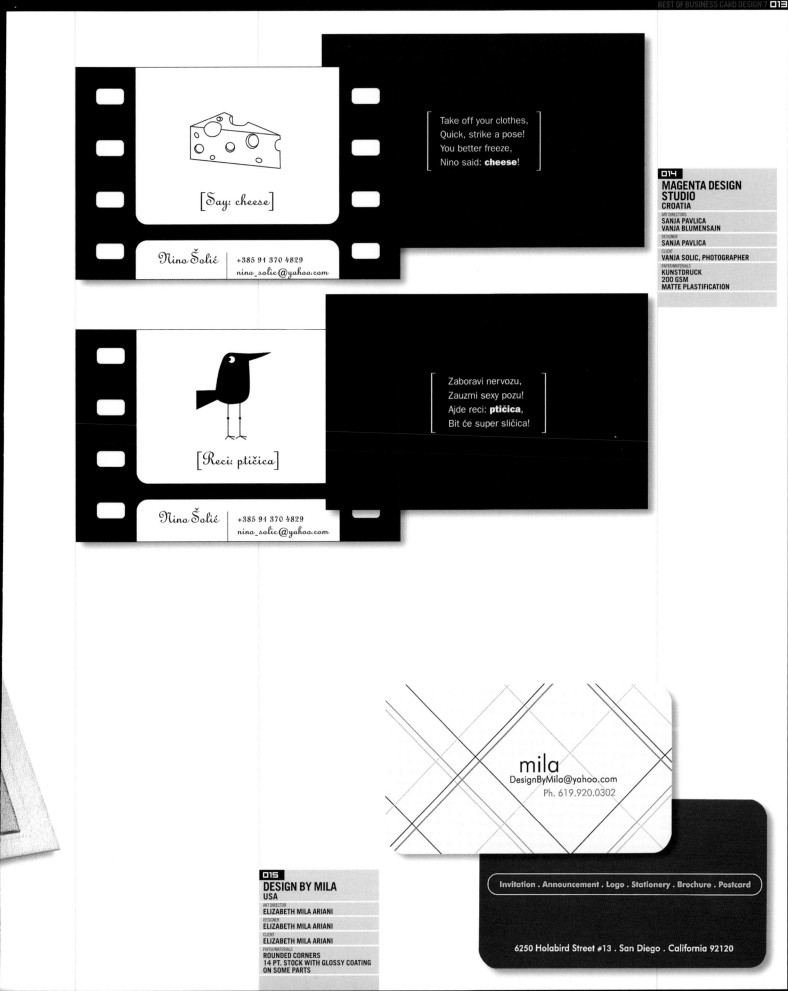

Take off your clothes,
Quick, strike a pose!
You better freeze,
Nino said: **cheese**!

[Say: cheese]

Nino Šolić   +385 91 370 4829
nino_solic@yahoo.com

Zaboravi nervozu,
Zauzmi sexy pozu!
Ajde reci: **ptičica**,
Bit će super sličica!

[Reci: ptičica]

Nino Šolić   +385 91 370 4829
nino_solic@yahoo.com

014
MAGENTA DESIGN STUDIO
CROATIA
ART DIRECTORS
SANJA PAVLICA
VANJA BLUMENSAJN
DESIGNER
SANJA PAVLICA
CLIENT
VANJA SOLIC, PHOTOGRAPHER
PAPER/MATERIALS
KUNSTDRUCK
200 GSM
MATTE PLASTIFICATION

mila
DesignByMila@yahoo.com
Ph. 619.920.0302

Invitation . Announcement . Logo . Stationery . Brochure . Postcard

6250 Holabird Street #13 . San Diego . California 92120

015
DESIGN BY MILA
USA
ART DIRECTOR
ELIZABETH MILA ARIANI
DESIGNER
ELIZABETH MILA ARIANI
CLIENT
ELIZABETH MILA ARIANI
PAPER/MATERIALS
ROUNDED CORNERS
14 PT. STOCK WITH GLOSSY COATING
ON SOME PARTS

FOOD
FOR THOUGHT

Events catered for
from **£3.50** per person

HOW'S
GYM
GOING?

Salads from **£2.95**

Aziz Hussein

2 Mitcham Road, Tooting
London SW17 9NA

T 020 8682 3444
M 07956 240 878

www.babosh.com
zizahussein@hotmail.com

BABOSH
Good food, freshly made

START A
DIET

(NEXT WEEK)

Cakes & pastries
from **90p**

016
ATELIER WORKS
UNITED KINGDOM
ART DIRECTOR
IAN CHILVERS
DESIGNER
JOSEPH LUFFMAN
CLIENT
BABOSH
PAPER/MATERIALS
300 GSM PRINTSPEED

Juliet Phillips

020 7761 9801
jp@k547.com

k547
Tregarvon Place
London
N1 3DY

018
LOEWY
UNITED KINGDOM
ART DIRECTOR
PAUL BURGESS
CLIENT
K547

IDEAS THAT MAKE THINGS HAPPEN.

S REILLY, Vice Pres

EET, SUITE E SAN DI

@tylerblik.com W

TYLER BLIK, Principal
655 G STREET, SUITE E SAN DIEGO, CA 92101 PH. 619.234.4434 FX. 619.234.4494
tyler@tylerblik.com WWW.TYLERBLIK.COM

017
BLIK
USA
ART DIRECTOR
TYLER BLIK
DESIGNER
KAY TODA
CLIENT
BLIK
PAPER/MATERIALS
STRATHMORE PURE COTTON

Arthur Collin, Partner
AA Dip B AppSc RIBA

DAAM 1a Berry Place
London EC1V 0JD
T +44 (0)20 7490 3520
F +44 (0)20 7490 3521
www.daam.co.uk
arthur@daam.co.uk

019
NB:STUDIO
UNITED KINGDOM
ART DIRECTOR
JODIE WIGHTMAN
CLIENT
DAAM

020
FITCH, SEATTLE
USA
ART DIRECTORS
STEVE WATSON
RAY UENO
DESIGNER
JASON GOMEZ
CLIENT
SCIENCE FICTION MUSEUM AND HALL
OF FAME
PAPER/MATERIALS
STRATHMORE ULTIMATE WHITE
110# PASTED COVER

Central Command
2901 Third Ave.
Suite 400
Seattle, WA 9812

Central Command
2901 Third Ave.
Suite 400
Seattle, WA 98121

MATT STUART SHOOTS PEOPLE

Matthew Stuart Photographer
67 Speed House Barbican London EC2Y 8AU
m +44 (0)7956 178690 t +44 (0)20 7628 8793
matt@mattstuart.com www.mattstuart.com

MATT STUART FRAMES STRANGERS

Matthew Stuart Photographer
67 Speed House Barbican London EC2Y 8AU
m +44 (0)7956 178690 t +44 (0)20 7628 8793
matt@mattstuart.com www.mattstuart.com

021
300MILLION
UNITED KINGDOM
ART DIRECTORS
DOM BAILEY
NIGEL DAVIES
MARTIN LAWLESS
DESIGNERS
DOM BAILEY
NIGEL DAVIES
MARTIN LAWLESS
CLIENT
MATT STUART

MATT STUART SNAPS LEGS

Matthew Stuart Photographer
67 Speed House Barbican London EC2Y 8AU
m +44 (0)7956 178690 t +44 (0)20 7628 8793
matt@mattstuart.com www.mattstuart.com

MATT STUART EXPOSES EVERYTHING

Matthew Stuart Photographer
67 Speed House Barbican London EC2Y 8AU
m +44 (0)7956 178690 t +44 (0)20 7628 8793
matt@mattstuart.com www.mattstuart.com

SFM.
SCIENCE FICTION MUSEUM
AND HALL OF FAME

o Contact:
T 206 SCI FICT
T 877 SCI FICT
F 206 770 2727
E info@sf

CI FICT
CI FICT
70 2727
sfhomeworld.org

nako

www.dimaquina.com

nako@dimaquina.com
55 21 25296140
55 21 87036657
skype: dimaquina

022
DIMAQUINA
BRAZIL

ART DIRECTORS
NAKO
DANIEL NEVES
ANTÔNIO PEDRO

DESIGNERS
NAKO
DANIEL NEVES
ANTÔNIO PEDRO

CLIENT
DIMAQUINA (SELF-PROMOTION)

PAPER/MATERIALS
YUPO PAPER (250 GSM)
SILKSCREEN

Aptos. Tenesor
Avda. de Tirajana
Playa del Ingles
Gran Canaria
Tel 928 761 063

Aptos. Tenesor
Avda. de Tirajana
Playa del Ingles
Gran Canaria
Tel 928 761 063

JONATHAN REED PRINCIPAL
SPEC ENTERTAINMENT

SPECENTERTAINMENT.COM **WWW.SPECENTERTAINMENT.COM**
MERCER STREET NEW YORK NY 10012 T 646 202 1820
ANGELES 1112 MONTANA AVENUE SUITE 305
310 868 1420 F 310 868 1422

SPEC

ENTERTAINMENT

024
GEYRHALTER DESIGN
USA
ART DIRECTOR
FABIAN GEYRHALTER
DESIGNERS
FABIAN GEYRHALTER
EVELYN KIM
CLIENT
SPEC ENTERTAINMENT

Aptos. Tenesor
Avda. de Tirajana
Playa del Ingles
Gran Canaria
Tel 928 761 063

023
ZIP DESIGN LTD.
UNITED KINGDOM
ART DIRECTOR
PETER CHADWICK
DESIGNER
PETER CHADWICK
CLIENT
MUNDO RESTAURANT

025

R&MAG GRAPHIC DESIGN
ITALY

ART DIRECTORS
FONTANELLA
DI SOMMA
CESAR

CLIENT
B-WHITE MULTISTORE

B-White
MULTISTORE

026

WERBE- &
MEDIEN-AKADEMIE
MARQUARDT—
SEÁN NAGEL
GERMANY

ART DIRECTOR
MARTIN SCHONHOFF

DESIGNER
SEÁN NAGEL

CLIENT
SEÁN NAGEL

PAPER/MATERIALS
250 GSM OFFSET

SEÁN MCCORMACK
GRAPHIC DESIGN

Bergmannstrasse 22
44145 Dortmund
Germany

Fon +49 231 2223430
Cell +49 160 4910808

sean@divingclown.com
divingclown.com

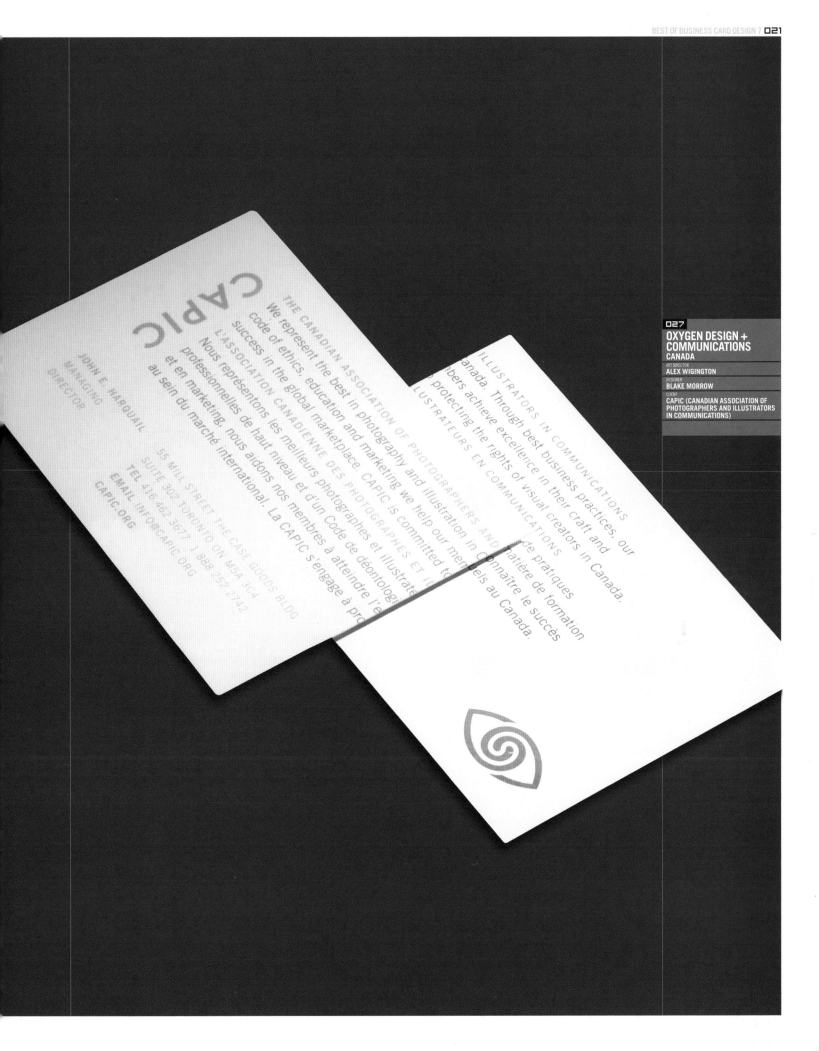

CAPIC

THE CANADIAN ASSOCIATION OF PHOTOGRAPHERS AND
We represent the best in photography and illustration in C
code of ethics, education and marketing we help our me
success in the global marketplace. CAPIC is committed to
L'ASSOCIATION CANADIENNE DES PHOTOGRAPHES ET IL
Nous représentons les meilleurs photographes et illustrate
professionnelles de haut niveau et d'un Code de déontologi
et en marketing, nous aidons nos membres à atteindre l'e
au sein du marché international. La CAPIC s'engage à pro

JOHN E. HARQUAIL
MANAGING
DIRECTOR

55 MILL STREET THE CASE GOODS BLDG
SUITE 302 TORONTO ON M5A 3C4
TEL 416.462.3677 1 888 252.2742
EMAIL INFO@CAPIC.ORG
CAPIC.ORG

ILLUSTRATORS IN COMMUNICATIONS
anada. Through best business practices, our
bers achieve excellence in their craft and
protecting the rights of visual creators in Canada.
LUSTRATEURS EN COMMUNICATIONS
de pratiques
atière de formation
nnaître le succès
els au Canada.

027

**OXYGEN DESIGN +
COMMUNICATIONS**
CANADA

ART DIRECTOR
ALEX WIGINGTON

DESIGNER
BLAKE MORROW

CLIENT
**CAPIC (CANADIAN ASSOCIATION OF
PHOTOGRAPHERS AND ILLUSTRATORS
IN COMMUNICATIONS)**

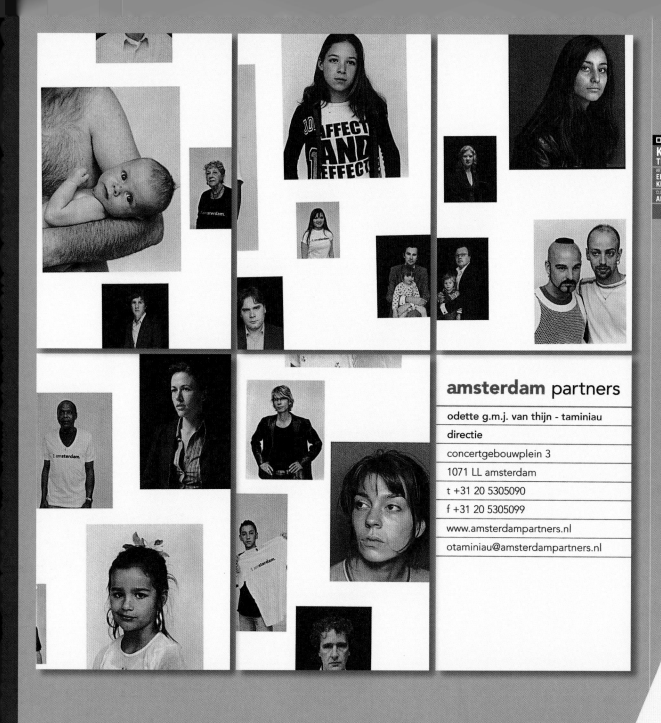

028
KESSELSKRAMER
THE NETHERLANDS
ART DIRECTORS
ERIK KESSELS
KRISTA ROZEMA
CLIENT
AMSTERDAM PARTNERS

amsterdam partners

odette g.m.j. van thijn - taminiau

directie

concertgebouwplein 3

1071 LL amsterdam

t +31 20 5305090

f +31 20 5305099

www.amsterdampartners.nl

otaminiau@amsterdampartners.nl

030
GOUTHIER DESIGN
USA
ART DIRECTOR
JONATHAN GOUTHIER
DESIGNER
JONATHAN GOUTHIER
CLIENT
BAND OF WRITERS

BAND MEMBER   Mike Giambattista

EM   mike@bandofwriters.net

LOCATION   2250 SW 28th Terrace   Fort Lauderdale, Florida 33312

PH   954 319-5000   FX   954 321-3291   WEB   www.bandofwriters.net

band of writers

029
TONIC DESIGN LTD.
UNITED KINGDOM
ART DIRECTORS
JAY PRYNNE
RANZIE ANTHONY
DESIGNER
JAY PRYNNE
CLIENT
PETR WEIGL
PAPER/MATERIALS
SPLENDORGEL 400 GSM

PETRWEIGL

Praha · London

032
MUGGIE RAMADANI
DESIGN STUDIO
DENMARK
ART DIRECTOR
MUGGIE RAMADANI
DESIGNER
MUGGIE RAMADANI
CLIENT
WAERUM

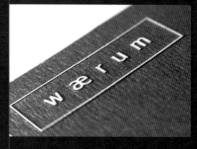

031
NANCY WU DESIGN
CANADA
ART DIRECTOR
NANCY WU
DESIGNER
NANCY WU
CLIENT
DR. WINNIE SU
PAPER/MATERIALS
FRASER PEGASUS
LITHO

蘇韻妮女西醫
BSc, MD, CCFP

家庭醫生及婦產科
Suite 250 . 2184 West Broadway Vancouver BC V6K 2E1
醫務所電話 604 733.5181

Dr. Winnie Su
BSc, MD, CCFP

FAMILY MEDICINE & OBSTETRICS
Suite 250 . 2184 West Broadway Vancouver BC V6K 2E1
T 604 733.5181 F 604 733.5184

PAM
ROHS

pam@the-joneses.com

1501 COLORADO AVENUE
SANTA MONICA CALIFORNIA 90404
T 310 656 8300 F 310 393 9696
www.the-joneses.com

034

PH.D
USA

ART DIRECTORS
CLIVE PIERCY
MICHAEL HODGSON

DESIGNERS
CLIVE PIERCY
JOHN HUGHES

CLIENT
THE JONESES

PAPER/MATERIALS
NEENAH CLASSIC CREST
SOLAR WHITE
130# COVER

ONE RUBBER BASE
TYPE: LINEAR / REF NO. 045A
BASE INTERIORS LTD

BASE

020 7487 3222
TEL. #

020 7487 3555
FAX. #

033

UNREAL
UNITED KINGDOM

ART DIRECTOR
BRIAN EAGLE

DESIGNER
BRIAN EAGLE

CLIENT
RICHARD BRAY, BASE INTERIORS

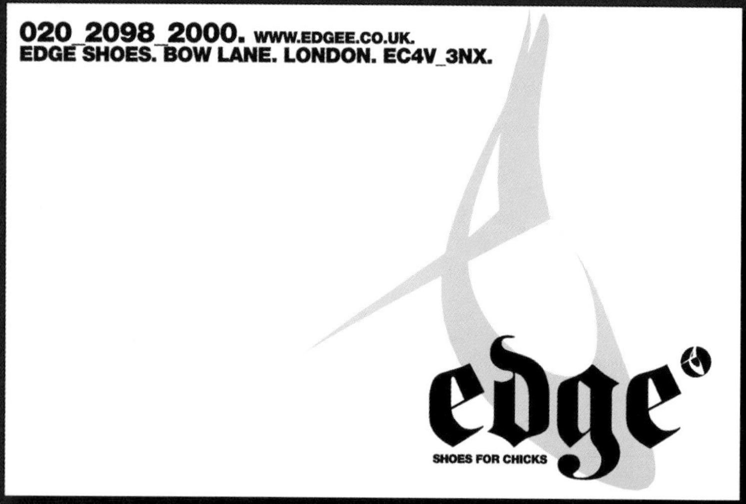

020_2098_2000. WWW.EDGEE.CO.UK.
EDGE SHOES. BOW LANE. LONDON. EC4V_3NX.

edge

SHOES FOR CHICKS

035
LOEWY
UNITED KINGDOM
ART DIRECTOR
PAUL BURGESS
CLIENT
EDGE SHOES

PETER HORNSBY

J2C DIESPEKER YARD
LONDON N1 4PJ
020 7761 9801
PETERH@J2C.COM

j2.C

JUST2CLICKS.COM

036
LOEWY
UNITED KINGDOM
ART DIRECTOR
PAUL BURGESS
CLIENT
JUST 2 CLICKS

SteersMcGillan Ltd
The Tobacco Factory
Bristol BS3 1TF
T: 0117 902 0444
F: 0117 902 0445

BRITISH MADE BRITISH MADE BRITISH MA

DOWNTOWN RADIATOR
& AUTOMOTIVE

MANAGER: Mark Garcia
LOCATION: 505 Fairview
Houston, Tx 77006
PHONE: 713.523.3546
713.524.3533
WEB: downtownradiator.com
EXPERTISE: A/C Specialist
Cooling System Specialist
40 Years of Experience

Chloë —
01179024466
Call me !

TISH MA

039
ZION GRAPHICS
SWEDEN
ART DIRECTOR
RICKY TILLBLAD
DESIGNER
RICKY TILLBLAD
CLIENT
PLAST I STOCKHOLM AB

plast™

SPECIAL EVENTS   MUSIC   VIDEO

NAME	TITLE
Joachim Hövel	Creative Director

ADDRESS	TEL & FAX	E-MAIL & WEB
Plast i Stockholm AB	Tel: +46 8 663 35 05	joachim@plast.se
Fryxellsgatan 3, 5th fl.	Fax: +46 8 663 35 80	www.plast.se
SE-114 25 Stockholm	Mob: +46 70 777 65 32	
Sweden		

Jimmy Fok photographer m 98586412

Calibre

213 Henderson Rd #02–01 Henderson Industrial Park Singapore 159553
p 65 6225 1005 f 65 6275 5845 e jimmy@calibrepics.com w calibrepics.com

01
02
03
04

0045 / 229 26 844, bache@mikkelbache.com, www.mikkelba

0045 / 229 26 844, bache@mikkelbache.com, w

041
MUGGIE RAMADANI
DESIGN STUDIO
DENMARK

ART DIRECTOR
MUGGIE RAMADANI

DESIGNER
MUGGIE RAMADANI

CLIENT
MIKKEL BACHE, PHOTOGRAPHER

040
KINETIC SINGAPORE
SINGAPORE

ART DIRECTORS
ROY POH
PANN LIM
LENG SOH

DESIGNER
LENG SOH

CLIENT
CALIBRE

PAPER/MATERIALS
SILKWIND WHITE 335 GSM

042

FFURIOUS
SINGAPORE

ART DIRECTOR
LITTLE ONG
DESIGNER
LITTLE ONG
CLIENT
LYN YAP
PAPER/MATERIALS
**250 GSM EAGLE SILHOUETTE
PREMIUM MATTE CARD
UV SPOT VARNISH**

PHOTOGRAPHER

[65] 8125 4324

LYN@LYNYAP.COM

WWW.LYNYAP.COM

REJANE DAL BELLO
graphic designer

BRAZIL // NETHERLAND
rejane@dalbello.com.br
www.dalbello.com.br/rejane

043

DAL BELLO
BRAZIL

ART DIRECTOR
REJANE DAL BELLO
DESIGNER
REJANE DAL BELLO
CLIENT
DAL BELLO
PAPER/MATERIALS
COURIOUS PAPER; ARJO WIGGINS

044
NINA DAVID
KOMMUNIKATIONSDESIGN
GERMANY
ART DIRECTOR
NINA DAVID
CLIENT
NINA DAVID KOMMUNIKATIONSDESIGN
PAPER/MATERIALS
SPLENDORGEL

www.ninadavid.de

pulling string

Pulling Strings believes in the quality of our labels and their designs. We carry a wide range of the most promising Asian labels, each of which has its own distinctive identity and creative direction. Should you wish to have a chat about our latest collection, feel free to contact Valerie Yeang by calling +65.9793 5509, faxing +65.6356.4763, or emailing valerie.yeang@pulling-strings.com. Alternatively, point your browser to www.pulling-strings.com and find out why you should pull this string.

PS001092004VY

045
KINETIC SINGAPORE
SINGAPORE
ART DIRECTORS
ROY POH
PANN LIM
LENG SOH
DESIGNER
LENG SOH
CLIENT
PULLING STRINGS
PAPER/MATERIALS
300 GSM GLOBAL PRINT ART
BOARD WITH NYLON STRING
AND SILVER EYELET

_m_bsc.architecture_aa.grad.dipl
architect+44(0)7973293885_ivaha@
_d.net_l.wingham@ukonline.co.uk_
_urer_university.of.greenwich
_33191128_l.wingham@gre.ac.uk_
_didate_the.bartlett.university.college_
l.wingham@ucl.ac.u

048
EDESIGN MEDIA
USA
ART DIRECTOR
DERRICK LEUNG
DESIGNER
DERRICK LEUNG
CLIENT
EDESIGN MEDIA
PAPER/MATERIALS
HEAVY SMOOTH SUBSTRATE (GREY)

[eDESIGNMEDIA]

GRAPHIC + PRINT + WEB DESIGN | E-COMMERCE

KUNIAKIMATSUDAIRA

KUNI@EDESIGNMEDIA.COM | www.edesignmedia.com

805 532 0891 | KUNI@EDESIGNMEDIA.COM

ALAN ALTMAN

Principal Creative Director

IDENTITY ANNUAL REPORTS
PACKAGING ADVERTISING

A3 DESIGN

W — | ATHREEDESIGN.COM | E· alan@athreedesign | 7809 CAUSEWAY DRIVE SUITE 207
(704) 568. 5351 TEL
· (704) 568. 5351 Fax | CHARLOTTE NORTH CAROLINA 28227

Ⓐ³

050
A3 DESIGN
USA
ART DIRECTOR
ALAN ALTMAN
DESIGNER
AMANDA ALTMAN
CLIENT
A3 DESIGN
PAPER/MATERIALS
**CLASSIC CREST
80# C SMOOTH
EMBER BLUE**

>> denis dulude
designer graphique

4623, Harvard   Montréal (Qc) H4A 2X3
T. 514.481.9735   C. 514.836.1961   F. 514.486.8657
denis@dulude.ca
AIM : denisdulude2

049
DULUDE
CANADA
ART DIRECTOR
DENIS DULUDE
DESIGNER
DENIS DULUDE
CLIENT
DULUDE
PAPER/MATERIALS
LETTERPRESS ON MOHAWK

DULUDE

Canfield Printing Inc.
137 Varick Street New York City 10013
212.206.9097 Fax: 206.0869 Email: CanPrint@aol.com

Stan Wolkoff

052
URETSKY + CO.
USA
ART DIRECTOR
JAN AUDUN URETSKY
DESIGNER
JAN AUDUN URETSKY
CLIENT
CANFIELD PRINTING INC.
PAPER/MATERIALS
OFFSET
STRATHMORE WHITE WOVE

SEÁN MCCORMACK
GRAPHIC DESIGN

Bergmannstrasse 22 | 44145 Dortmund | Germany
Fon +49 231 2223430 | Cell +49 160 4910808
sean@divingclown.com | divingclown.com

051
**WERBE- &
MEDIEN-AKADEMIE
MARQUARDT—
SEÁN NAGEL**
GERMANY
ART DIRECTOR
MARTIN SCHONHOFF
DESIGNER
SEÁN NAGEL
CLIENT
SEÁN NAGEL
PAPER/MATERIALS
250 GSM OFFSET

053

R&MAG GRAPHIC DESIGN
ITALY
ART DIRECTORS
FONTANELLA
DI SOMMA
CESAR
CLIENT
ZOOLAB

Oreste Palmieri

ZooLab di Vincenzo Cuomo sas
via del Pescatore 3
80053 Castellammare di Stabia (Na)
telefono e fax 081 3915489
partita iva 03969801210

http://www.zoolab.it
info@zoolab.it

ZOO:LAB
New media agency
Systems integrator

009°10'47 E
048°46'59 N

t 0711 . 231 68 82
f 0711 . 231 68 83

bravo charlie · lautenschlagerstraße 14 · 70173 stuttgart
alpha@bravo-charlie.de www.bravo-charlie.de

054

I_D BUERO GMBH
GERMANY
ART DIRECTORS
OLIVER–A. KRIMMEL
ANJA OSTERWALDER
DESIGNERS
CHRISTINE DORST
PIA BARDESONO
CLIENT
BRAVO CHARLIE GMBH
PAPER/MATERIALS
INVERCOTE CREATO MATTE 350 GSM

055
VISUELLE
KOMMUNIKATION
GERMANY
DIRECTOR
HEIKE HARMANN
CLIENT
RAUMAUSSTATTUNG CLAUS

Raumausstattung Claus
Fensterdekorationen | Sonnenschutz | Bodenbeläge
Polsterwerkstatt

Annette Claus
Bornheimer Landwehr 57 | 60385 Frankfurt am Main
Telefon 069. 44 64 81 | Telefax 069. 43 30 87
T-Mobil 0170. 4 43 70 64 | E-Mail A_Claus @ t-online.de

william fritts
president

intelligent d

intelligent

056
PLAZM
USA
ART DIRECTORS
JOSHUA BERGER
PETE MCCRACKEN
DESIGNERS
JOSHUA BERGER
PETE MCCRACKEN
CLIENT
INTELLIGENT DESIGN
PAPER/MATERIALS
PRINTED ON RUBBERIZED STOCK
ALL STATIONERY INDIVIDUALLY SEALED

057

BASE ART CO.
USA
ART DIRECTOR
TERRY ROHRBACH
DESIGNER
TERRY ROHRBACH
CLIENT
BASE ART CO.
PAPER/MATERIALS
OPUS 100# DULL COVER

A GRAPHIC DESIGN STUDIO

BASE ART CO.

TERRY ROHRBACH
BASE ART CO. 623 HIGH STREET
WORTHINGTON OH 43085
T 614 841 7480 F 614 841 7481
TBACH@BASEARTCO.COM
WWW.BASEARTCO.COM

ēthos
watch studio
+91 1725 48223   www.ethoswatches.com

yasho saboo ceo

058

ICONTRACT
INDIA
ART DIRECTOR
VIJU MENON
DESIGNER
AVINASH NAMADHARI
CLIENT
ETHOS WATCH STUDIOS
PAPER/MATERIALS
RIVES TRADITION BRIGHT WHITE

060

STYLOROUGE
UNITED KINGDOM

ART DIRECTOR
ROB O'CONNOR

DESIGNER
ROB O'CONNOR

CLIENT
UNCONVENTIONAL PRODUCTIONS

PAPER/MATERIALS
CARD

059

DIMENSI + GRAPHIC DESIGN
INDONESIA

ART DIRECTOR
JOHN GUNAWAN

DESIGNER
JOHN GUNAWAN

CLIENT
DIMENSI + GRAPHIC DESIGN

PAPER/MATERIALS
HVS PAPER 85 GRAM
SILVER PAPER
DUPLEX BOARD

PRINTING COMPANY
KANOMAN PRINTING

Custom Urethane Castings

CUSTOM
MOLD MAKING

Josh Christie
316 619 3629

HOTROD
SHIFT KNOBS

Dennis Rooney
316 651 7713

FUNKY
PAINT JOBS

WWW.VANCHASE.COM

VAN CHASE

061
UP DESIGN BUREAU
USA
ART DIRECTOR
CHRIS PARKS
DESIGNER
CHRIS PARKS
CLIENT
JOSH CHRISTIE
PAPER/MATERIALS
COUGAR 100#

Mike Campbell
FUZZY@TSTAR.NET

TEL 830♦598♦6998
CEL 512♦567♦5661
FAX 830♦598♦4137

POST OFFICE BOX 4308 ♦ 1307 MOUNTAIN DEW
♦ HORSESHOE BAY ♦ TEXAS ♦ USA ♦ 78657

062
UP DESIGN BUREAU
USA
ART DIRECTOR
CHRIS PARKS
DESIGNER
CHRIS PARKS
CLIENT
MIKE CAMPBELL
PAPER/MATERIALS
COUGAR 100#

Fat Fenders

MOBILE
Soda
BLASTING

AL FLEMING

www.fatfenderssodablasting-com
316♦990♦1420
JACKET EMBLEMS

email al@fatfenderssodablasting·com

Mobile SODA BLASTING

063
UP DESIGN BUREAU
USA
ART DIRECTOR
CHRIS PARKS
DESIGNER
CHRIS PARKS
CLIENT
AL FLEMING
PAPER/MATERIALS
COUGAR 100#

MOTO SUGAI ► 316.390.4964 ► MOTONARIS@HOTMAIL.COM

MOTO SUGAI

064
UP DESIGN BUREAU
USA
ART DIRECTOR
CHRIS PARKS
DESIGNER
CHRIS PARKS
CLIENT
MOTO SUGAI
PAPER/MATERIALS
COUGAR 100#

065
UP DESIGN BUREAU
USA
ART DIRECTOR
CHRIS PARKS
DESIGNER
CHRIS PARKS
CLIENT
MITCH WILLIS — GO AWAY GARAGE
PAPER/MATERIALS
COUGAR 100#

066
9MYLES, INC.
USA
ART DIRECTOR
MYLES MCGUINNESS
DESIGNER
MYLES MCGUINNESS
CLIENT
BRAND SLAM
PAPER/MATERIALS
CLASSIC CREST/CREAM; 120# COVER

067
UP DESIGN BUREAU
USA
ART DIRECTOR
CHRIS PARKS
DESIGNER
CHRIS PARKS
CLIENT
MARILYN CAMPBELL
PAPER/MATERIALS
COUGAR 100#

068
UP DESIGN BUREAU
USA
ART DIRECTOR
CHRIS PARKS
DESIGNER
CHRIS PARKS
CLIENT
MITCH WILLIS
PAPER/MATERIALS
COUGAR 100#

Do you expect
me to talk?

No, no Mr Bond.
I expect you to
marmalade©

Don't worry Mr B,
I have a cunning
marmalade©

We came, we saw,
we kicked its
marmalade©

At my signal...
unleash
marmalade©

Andy Cutbill

Mobile +44 (0)7841 576 000
Landline +44 (0)20 8846 3731
andy@marmaladecreative.co.uk
www.marmaladecreative.co.uk

Marmalade Creative
The Courtyard
42 Colwith Road
London W6 0EY
United Kingdom

star99.1**FM**
Today's Christian Music

» scott@star991fm.com
» 732.469.0991
» 732.469.2115 fax
» P.O. Box 9058
Zarephath, NJ 08890-9058
Scott Taylor   » www.star991fm.com
Program Director *Pillar of Fire International*

070
**3RD EDGE
COMMUNICATIONS**
USA
ART DIRECTOR
FRANKIE GONZALEZ
DESIGNER
FRANKIE GONZALEZ
CLIENT
STAR 99.1 FM

071
**OTHERWISE
INCORPORATED**
USA
ART DIRECTORS
**DAVID FREJ (CREATIVE DIRECTOR)
TODD JONES (ART DIRECTOR)**
DESIGNER
TODD JONES
CLIENT
OTHERWISE INCORPORATED
PAPER/MATERIALS
**120# SAPPI STROBE DULL COVER
2 PMS + SGV/4C PROCESS + 1 PMS +
OAGV**

OTHERWISE INCORPORATED

TODD JONES | ART DIRECTOR
1144 WEST RANDOLPH STREET | CHICAGO, ILLINOIS 60607
T. 312 226 1144 | F. 312 226 3836 | TJONES@OTHERWISEINC.COM

RICHARD BURGESS
ARCHITECT

072
LOEWY
UNITED KINGDOM
ART DIRECTOR
PAUL BURGESS
CLIENT
K ONE

JUBURGE HOUSE. PIPS COURT. LONDON. SW12 9LG.
T. +44 (0)20 8673 6900. M. +44 (0)7976 601790
www.k-one-uk.net. richard@k-one-uk.net

me, me

hellomeme.com

fiel valdez, peter vattanatham

me, me

hellomeme.com

fiel valdez, peter vattanatham

073

ME, ME
USA

ART DIRECTORS
**PETER VATTANATHAM
FIEL VALDEZ**

DESIGNERS
**PETER VATTANATHAM
FIEL VALDEZ**

CLIENT
ME, ME

fast
setting
efficient
festive
evening
gourmet
outdoor
trendy

רועי גוזמן   +972(3)6129333
+972(66)646577
+972(3)6129565

ego

MOBILE FOOD

grilled
cocktails
fresh
barbeque
tasty
dinner
service

setting
efficient
festive
evening
gourmet
outdoor
trendy

+972(3)6129333
+972(3)6129565

ego

MOBILE FOOD

grilled
cocktails
fresh
barbeque
tasty
dinner
service

074

TAMAR MANY AND YANEK IONTEF
ISRAEL

ART DIRECTORS
**TAMAR MANY
YANEK IONTEF**

DESIGNER
**TAMAR MANY
YANEK IONTEF**

CLIENT
EGO MOBILE FOOD

PAPER/MATERIALS
SILKSCREEN ON CARDBOARD PAPER

075

MAYHEM MEDIA
USA
DESIGNER
ERIC HINES
CLIENT
STEVE HARRIS
PAPER/MATERIALS
CLASSIC CREST DUPLEX

STEVE HARRIS PHOTOGRAPHY
steve@steveharrisphoto.com

713.222.7373

mori:projects

Innenarchitektur

Claudia·Wald········Lortzingweg·12·········71032·Böblingen
t··07031.239 122·······f··07031.239 121·················
wald@mori-projects.de···············www.mori-projects.de

076

STILRADAR
GERMANY
ART DIRECTORS
RAPHAEL POHLAND
SIMONE WINTER
CLIENT
MORI-PROJECTS

077
DAVID ROJAS
MEXICO
DESIGNER
DAVID ROJAS
CLIENT
V2 – PHOTO
PAPER/MATERIALS
PREMIUM; 8016; 215 GSM; MATTE

[+] vision 2]   [[   ]

t. 044 (55) 2313 • 7210 / 56 16 39 _38
www.v2-photo.com / info@v2-photo.com

7903 Greenwood Ave. N.
Seattle. WA 98103

Robynn

7903 Greenwood Ave. N.
Seattle, WA 98103

T 206 789-7667
F 206 789-3171

moderndog.co
vito@modernd

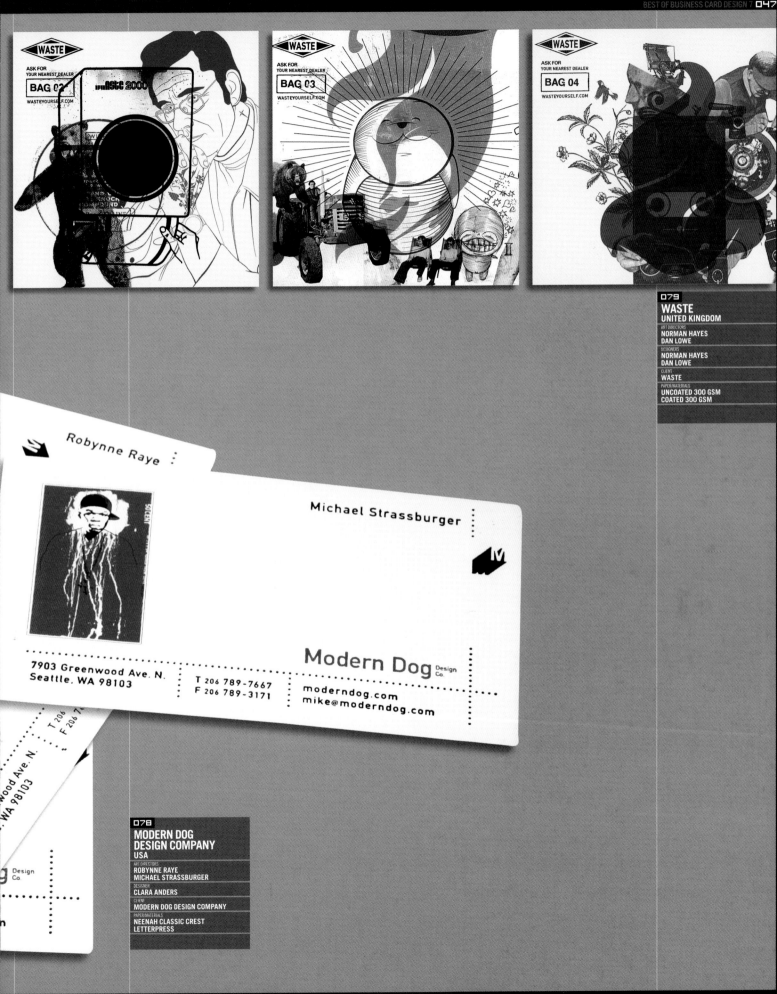

WASTE
ASK FOR
YOUR NEAREST DEALER
BAG 02
WASTEYOURSELF.COM

WASTE
ASK FOR
YOUR NEAREST DEALER
BAG 03
WASTEYOURSELF.COM

WASTE
ASK FOR
YOUR NEAREST DEALER
BAG 04
WASTEYOURSELF.COM

079
WASTE
UNITED KINGDOM

ART DIRECTORS
**NORMAN HAYES
DAN LOWE**

DESIGNERS
**NORMAN HAYES
DAN LOWE**

CLIENT
WASTE

PAPER/MATERIALS
**UNCOATED 300 GSM
COATED 300 GSM**

Robynne Raye

Michael Strassburger

Modern Dog Design Co.

7903 Greenwood Ave. N.
Seattle. WA 98103

T 206 789-7667
F 206 789-3171

moderndog.com
mike@moderndog.com

078
MODERN DOG
DESIGN COMPANY
USA

ART DIRECTORS
**ROBYNNE RAYE
MICHAEL STRASSBURGER**

DESIGNER
CLARA ANDERS

CLIENT
MODERN DOG DESIGN COMPANY

PAPER/MATERIALS
**NEENAH CLASSIC CREST
LETTERPRESS**

080

MUGGIE RAMADANI
DESIGN STUDIO
DENMARK

ART DIRECTOR
MUGGIE RAMADANI

DESIGNER
MUGGIE RAMADANI

CLIENT
PORTE À GAUCHE

081

HARRIMANSTEEL
UNITED KINGDOM

ART DIRECTOR
HARRIMANSTEEL

DESIGNER
HARRIMANSTEEL

CLIENT
ASD LIONHEART / BURGER

PAPER/MATERIALS
RAFLATAC RAFLAGLOSS

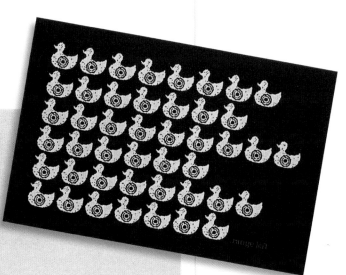

wesley anson

designer

07966 500 509

082
WES ANSON DESIGN
UNITED KINGDOM
ART DIRECTOR
WES ANSON
DESIGNER
WES ANSON
CLIENT
WES ANSON
PAPER/MATERIALS
GF SMITH UNCOATED WHITE
1-SIDE SATIN VARNISH

083
KEARNEYROCHOLL
GERMANY
ART DIRECTOR
FRANK ROCHOLL
DESIGNER
FRANK ROCHOLL
CLIENT
VIVIDPROJECTS
PAPER/MATERIALS
CHROMOLUX PLUS PANTONE METALLIC

Burger™

Burger™ Burger™

Burger™ Burger™ Burger™

Burger™ Burger™ Burger™ Burger™

Burger™ Burger™ Burger™ Burger™

don, W1F 8DN. T: 020 7663 2522. F: 020 7287 2150.

n.com

vividprojects™

084
ZIP DESIGN LTD.
UNITED KINGDOM
ART DIRECTOR
PETER CHADWICK
DESIGNER
HANNAH WOODCOCK
CLIENT
ZIP DESIGN LTD.
PAPER/MATERIALS
355 GSM WHITE IVORY BOARD

085
NB:STUDIO
UNITED KINGDOM
ART DIRECTORS
BEN STOTT
NICK VINCENT
CLIENT
HUH

The centre
for craft design
and making

Navigation Wharf
Carre Street
Sleaford
Lincolnshire NG34 7TW
United Kingdom

Tel +44 (0)1529 308710
susie.oreilly@
leisureconnection.co.uk

Susie O'Reilly
Education Consultant

086
NIKET PAREKH
INDIA
DESIGNER
NIKET PAREKH
CLIENT
ASHUTOSH PARIKH
PAPER/MATERIALS
KENTEX 330 GSM

ASHUTOSH PARIKH
9820 6889

ASHUTOSH PARIKH
9820 6889

LOUDSPEAKER MANUFACTURERS

087
NB:STUDIO
UNITED KINGDOM
ART DIRECTOR
ALAN DYE
CLIENT
NINCOMSOUP

NIN COM CO SOU

NIN COM SOUP SOU

NI CO SO SOUP

Nincomsoup
5-7 St Agnes Well
Old Street Station
London EC1Y 1BE
T 020 7490 4635
F 020 7250 3142

www.nincomsoup.co.uk
enquiries@nincomsoup.co.uk
order@nincomsoup.co.uk
recruitment@nincomsoup.co.uk

Soups Salads Wraps Bagels
Cakes Juices Coffee
Food for the discerning palate

KESSELSKRAMER
THE NETHERLANDS
ART DIRECTOR
ERIK KESSELS
CLIENT
KESSELSKRAMER

greg samata director
101 south first street dundee il 60118

noisemaker films

847 902 8601 C   847 426 4440 O

www.noisemakerfilms.com

SAMATAMASON
CANADA
ART DIRECTOR
GREG SAMATA
DESIGNER
GREG SAMATA
CLIENT
NOISEMAKER FILMS
PAPER/MATERIALS
134# COVER CRANES FLUORESCENT WHITE (TWO PIECES LINKED TOGETHER)

020 7794 2300   14 adam street
london
W1 1PE

MANDRAKE

LOEWY
UNITED KINGDOM
ART DIRECTOR
PAUL BURGESS
CLIENT
MANDRAKE CLUB

091
BLOK DESIGN
MEXICO

ART DIRECTOR
VANESSA ECKSTEIN

DESIGNERS
VANESSA ECKSTEIN
FRANCES CHEN

CLIENT
THE PRODUCTION KITCHEN

PAPER/MATERIALS
BENEFIT

THE PRODUCTION KITCHEN

49 SPADINA AVENUE Nº **506** TORONTO ON M5V 2J1

T: 416 599 1847 ext.223 F: 416 599 9829 C: 416 464 0160

RUTH GAUTHIER

FOR
RESULTS
IN PRINT

andrijana milanović

modni dizajner

milanović

011 34 73 203

017 41 44 11

092
THNK MARKETING
SERBIA & MONTENEGRO

ART DIRECTOR
PREDRAG MATOVIC

DESIGNER
PREDRAG MATOVIC

CLIENT
AM ANDRIJANA MILANOVIC –
FASHION DESIGN STUDIO

PAPER/MATERIALS
150 GSM PAPER; WHITE TREAD

093
Q
GERMANY
ART DIRECTOR
THILO VON DEBSCHITZ
DESIGNER
MARCEL KUMMERER
CLIENT
KSF – KARIN SCHMIDT-FRIDERICHS

094
LOEWY
UNITED KINGDOM
ART DIRECTOR
PAUL BURGESS
CLIENT
MANDRAKE CLUB

PERRY CHUA
CREATIVE DIRECTOR

1·866·877·4034 Tagline
PERRY@WOWBRANDING.COM

>>

W•O•W
BRANDING

096
WOW BRANDING
CANADA
ART DIRECTOR
PERRY CHUA
DESIGNERS
WILL JOHNSON
JEFF SCHRAMM
CLIENT
GLIMAC ENGINEERS
MATERIALS
100# MOHAWK NAVAJO

214 **528-3322** tel
528-3353 fax

3511 Hall Street, № 109
Dallas, Texas 75219

Ryan Gagnard
ryan@slantdesign.com

www.slantdesign.com

slant

095
SLANT, INC.
USA
ART DIRECTORS
DAVID SLACK
RYAN GAGNARD
DESIGNER
RYAN GAGNARD
CLIENT
SLANT

097
IMAGINE
UNITED KINGDOM
ART DIRECTOR
DAVID CAUNCE
DESIGNER
DAVID CAUNCE
CLIENT
FIDO PR
PAPER/MATERIALS
300 GSM IVORY BOARD
MATTE LAMINATION

Mandy Sharpe

fido

IPR
Members
Committed to Professionalism
The Institute of Public Relations

Fido Public Relations Limited
The Stables Paradise Wharf Ducie Street Manchester M1 2JN
Telephone **0161 274 3311** Facsimile **0161 273 1550**
Web **www.trustfido.co.uk** Email **mandy@trustfido.co.uk**

SparkyDesign

Sarah Kelsey
Art Director

600 E. 73rd Street
Kansas City, MO 64131

Studio: 816.523.0641
Mobile: 913.481.6630
sarah@sparkydesign.com

098
SPARKY DESIGN
USA
DESIGNER
SARAH KELSEY
CLIENT
SPARKY DESIGN
PAPER/MATERIALS
4/4 OFFSET

Collateral
Identity
Interactive
Packaging
Direct Mail

SparkyDesign
sparkydesign.com

099
RULE29
USA
ART DIRECTOR
JUSTIN AHRENS
DESIGNER
JUSTIN AHRENS
CLIENT
JIM CRAIG
PAPER/MATERIALS
NEENAH CLASSIC CREST

100
ENTERMOTION
DESIGN STUDIO
USA
ART DIRECTORS
BRIAN CARTWRIGHT
JOE MORROW
DESIGNER
LEA CARMICHAEL
CLIENT
CHAIRBRAIN
PAPER/MATERIALS
COUGAR OPAQUE SMOOTH

101
**MUGGIE RAMADANI
DESIGN STUDIO**
DENMARK

ART DIRECTOR
MUGGIE RAMADANI

DESIGNER
MUGGIE RAMADANI

CLIENT
TEEDOT

103
DESIGNKARMA INC.
USA

ART DIRECTOR
VITALLY YASCH

DESIGNER
TIMOFEL YOURIEV

CLIENT
DESIGNKARMA INC.

PAPER/MATERIALS
**STRATHMORE TRANSLUCENT
VELLUM 30# 111 GSM**

04
smarter**business**
3rd/4th/5th June 2004

»

102
LOEWY
UNITED KINGDOM

ART DIRECTOR
PAUL BURGESS

CLIENT
SMARTER BUSINESS

Ben **Brownlow**
Earls Court
London
W4 8PJ

07798 **607128**

BLOK DESIGN
MEXICO

ART DIRECTOR
VANESSA ECKSTEIN

DESIGNERS
VANESSA ECKSTEIN
STEPHANIE YOUNG

CLIENT
BEDLAM FILMS

PAPER/MATERIALS
STRATHMORE ULTIMATE WHITE

bedlam films

53 ONTARIO ST. TORONTO ON CANADA M5A 2V1 **T** 416 214 4525 **F** 416 869 1737

BEDLAM FILMS

BEDLAM FILMS 53 ONTARIO ST. TORONTO ON CANADA M5A 2V1
TEL: 416 214 4525 **FAX:** 416 869 1737 **CELL:** 416 917 2934

EVELYN ARTHUR

SHERRI VALENTI
PRESIDENT
DESIGN KARMA, INC.
PO BOX #1607
NEW YORK

DESIGNKARMA INC.
BASED IN NEW YORK CITY, DESIGN KARMA PROVIDES INTEGRATED
MARKETING AND DESIGN SERVICES THAT ENCOMPASS FULL-SCALE
CREATIVE SOLUTIONS. OUR SERVICES RANGE FROM INITIAL
CONCEPTING, BRAND DEVELOPMENT, MESSAGING AND STRATEGY, TO
ONGOING COMMUNICATIONS AND CREATIVE EXECUTION.

design·karma

Gayle Zalduondo
gzalduondo@urbanusfurniture.com

URBANUS
305/576-9510 ext 101
305/576-4735 fax

89 northeast 27 street miami, fl 33137

www.urbanusfurniture.com

106
INKBYTE DESIGN
USA
ART DIRECTOR
PETER ROMAN
DESIGNER
PETER ROMAN
CLIENT
URBANUS FURNITURE
PAPER/MATERIALS
EMBOSS
COPPER FOIL
DIE-CUT

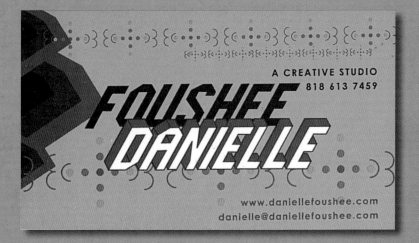

A CREATIVE STUDIO
818 613 7459

FOUSHÉE
DANIELLE

www.daniellefoushee.com
danielle@daniellefoushee.com

105
DANIELLE FOUSHÉE
DESIGN
USA
ART DIRECTOR
DANIELLE FOUSHÉE
DESIGNER
DANIELLE FOUSHÉE
CLIENT
DANIELLE FOUSHÉE
PAPER/MATERIALS
ADOBE ILLUSTRATOR
ADOBE INDESIGN

ALAN WILLS
alanwills@mentalgear.com

118 Ava Drive
Hewitt, Texas 76643

T 254 420.1010
F 254 420.1301

mentalgear.com

mentalgear.com

107

MODERN DOG
DESIGN COMPANY
USA

ART DIRECTOR
ROBYNNE RAYE

DESIGNER
ROBYNNE RAYE

CLIENT
MENTAL

PAPER/MATERIALS
DIGITAL PRINTING 4/4

KEVIN FUNG
514.892.5880

OISHII SUSHI

108

ZENDEN
CANADA

ART DIRECTOR
KEVIN FUNG

DESIGNERS
**KEVIN FUNG
MINH**

CLIENT
OISHII SUSHI

PAPER/MATERIALS
MATTE LUMINATE PAPER

109
ZIP DESIGN LTD.
UNITED KINGDOM
ART DIRECTOR
PETER CHADWICK
DESIGNER
HANNAH WOODCOCK
CLIENT
VINNIE ADVERTISING

Tim North
M +44 (0) 7764 964086
tim@vinnieadvertising.com

Vinnie
Pinewood Studios
Pinewood Road
Iver Heath
Bucks SL0 0NH

T +44 (0) 1753 654736
F +44 (0) 1753 653561
www.vinnieadvertising.com

110
IMAGINE
UNITED KINGDOM
ART DIRECTOR
DAVID CAUNCE
DESIGNER
DAVID CAUNCE
CLIENT
THE WHITE PEG LAUNDRY CO.
PAPER/MATERIALS
CONQUEROR CX22

THE **WHITE PEG**
LAUNDRY C°

LOUISE WATSON
PROPRIETOR

THE WHITE PEG LAUNDRY COMPANY
110-112 TIB STREET MANCHESTER M4 1LR
TELEPHONE **0161 834 5534**

arterium

David Shakeshaft

219 Oakwood Lane
2 Hollin Hill House
Leeds LS8 2PE

tel/fax 0113 240 3008
mobile 07710 601 913

e david@arterium.co.uk
w www.arterium.co.uk

111

EGGERS + DIAPER
GERMANY

ART DIRECTOR
BIRGIT EGGERS

DESIGNER
BIRGIT EGGERS

CLIENT
QUASI FOTOGRAFIE

112

THOMPSON
UNITED KINGDOM

ART DIRECTOR
IAN THOMPSON

DESIGNER
DAVID THOMPSON

CLIENT
ARTERIUM

PAPER/MATERIALS
**CONQUEROR DIAMOND WHITE WOVE
300 GSM**

113

STEERSMCGILLAN
UNITED KINGDOM

ART DIRECTOR
RICHARD MCGILLAN

DESIGNER
RICHARD MCGILLAN

CLIENT
THE STUDY GALLERY, POOLE

PAPER/MATERIALS
500 GSM BOARD

110° E
AT THE STUDY GALLERY, POOLE

150° SE
AT THE STUDY GALLERY, POOLE

140° SE
AT THE STUDY GALLERY, POOLE

200° S
AT THE STU

Staff

AT THE STUDY GALLERY, POOLE

The Study Gallery, The College, North Road, Poole, Dorset BH14 0LS
Tel-Fax: 01202 205200 Minicom: 01202 205225
Email: info@thestudygallery.org Web: thestudygallery.org

Anne Zangara
Creative Director, Corporate Design
Brand Management & Promotion

PBS

1320 Braddock Place Alexandria, VA 22314.1698
T.703.739.5006 F.703.739.5069
azangara@pbs.org

114

PBS CORPORATE DESIGN
USA

ART DIRECTOR
ANNA ZANGARA

DESIGNERS
ANNA ZANGARA
CARRIE WILLRICH
CHRISTOPHER RICHARD

CLIENT
PBS (PUBLIC BROADCASTING SERVICE)

PAPER/MATERIALS
STARWHITE COVER PLUS TIARA #88

engaged

Be more

original

Be more **PBS**

creative

honest

Be mor

original

engaged

115

STILRADAR
GERMANY
ART DIRECTORS
RAPHAEL POHLAND
SIMONE WINTER
CLIENT
REIZ BRILLEN

REIZ

Telephone +49 7153 36328   Facsimile +49 7153 36329

Jochen Gutbrod   General Director

Adress   REIZ   Borsigstraße 26   73249 Wernau   Germany

AUTHENTIC BRAND DESIGN
9MYLES INC
MYLES MCGUINNESS Creative Director   P] 858.344.8619
EST. 1998

☐ REGULAR ☐ PLUS ☑ PREMIUM

116

9MYLES, INC.
USA
ART DIRECTOR
MYLES MCGUINNESS
DESIGNER
MYLES MCGUINNESS
CLIENT
9MYLES, INC.
PAPER/MATERIALS
ALUMINUM METAL
VHS PAPER LABELS

117
ENLIGHTENMENT
JAPAN
ART DIRECTOR
ENLIGHTENMENT
DESIGNER
ENLIGHTENMENT
CLIENT
KAZE TO BALLAD INC.
PAPER/MATERIALS
MRS-B (JAPANESE PAPER)

LEEDS COLLEGE OF MUSIC

3 Quarry Hill
Leeds LS2 7PD
Tel: 0113 222 3400
Fax: 0113 243 8798
Email:
enquiries@lcm.ac.uk
www.lcm.ac.uk

David Warren
Director of development
d.warren@lcm.ac.uk
Mobile: 07703 345448

LCM

118

THOMPSON
UNITED KINGDOM

ART DIRECTOR
IAN THOMPSON

DESIGNER
DAVID THOMPSON

CLIENT
LEEDS COLLEGE OF MUSIC

PAPER/MATERIALS
**SKY UNCOATED BRILLIANT
WHITE 300 GSM**

119

**WERBE- &
MEDIEN-AKADEMIE
MARQUARDT−NINA
WIESENBERGER**
GERMANY

ART DIRECTOR
MARTIN SCHONHOFF

DESIGNER
NINA WIESENBERGER

CLIENT
JAN VON PUYVELDE

PAPER/MATERIALS
250 GSM PLAIN WHITE

lovecard PUI PUI

JAN VAN PUYVELDE   BUCHENSTRASSE 48   59423 UNNA
FON 02303−89143   MOBIL 0177−4238935   PUI.PUI@T-ONLINE.DE

to
cultivate

garden design

David Brandon
121B Highbury New Park, London N5 2HG
M:07816 904 108 T:020 7288 1715
E:david@tocultivate.com, www.tocultivate.com

plantworks

contemporary art

Karen Reade **01223 870 560**
Diana Nelson **01223 356 691**
46 Victoria Park, Cambridge, CB4 3EL
www.plantworks.uk.com

122

LOEWY
UNITED KINGDOM

ART DIRECTOR
PAUL BURGESS

CLIENT
MANDRAKE CLUB

020 7794 2300   14 adam street
london
W1 1PE

MANDRAKE

Steve Straus, P.E.
President
LEED® Accredited Professional

sstraus@

10419 Old Placerville R
Sacramento, CA 958

GLIMAC

engineers for a sustainable future

123

WOW BRANDING
CANADA

ART DIRECTOR
PERRY CHUA

DESIGNERS
WILL JOHNSON
JEFF SCHRAMM

CLIENT
GLIMAC ENGINEERS

MATERIALS
100# MOHAWK NAVAJO
581A.BC7 DIE CUT

S56

NAME   Henrik Steiner

ADDRESS   S56 Recordings AB
Majorsgatan 11
SE-114 47 Stockholm
PHONE   +46 8 667 55 00
FAX   +46 8 667 56 06
DIRECT   +46 8 528 029 08
E-MAIL   henrik@s56.com
WEB   www.s56.com

124
ZION GRAPHICS
SWEDEN
ART DIRECTOR
RICKY TILLBLAD
DESIGNER
RICKY TILLBLAD
CLIENT
556 RECORDINGS

martin kerslake //

kflake@hotmail.com **8079**
023 telephone 0935

36 sandringham lane // fair oak // hampshire //so42 8ky

125
LOEWY
UNITED KINGDOM
ART DIRECTOR
PAUL BURGESS
CLIENT
MARTIN KERSLAKE

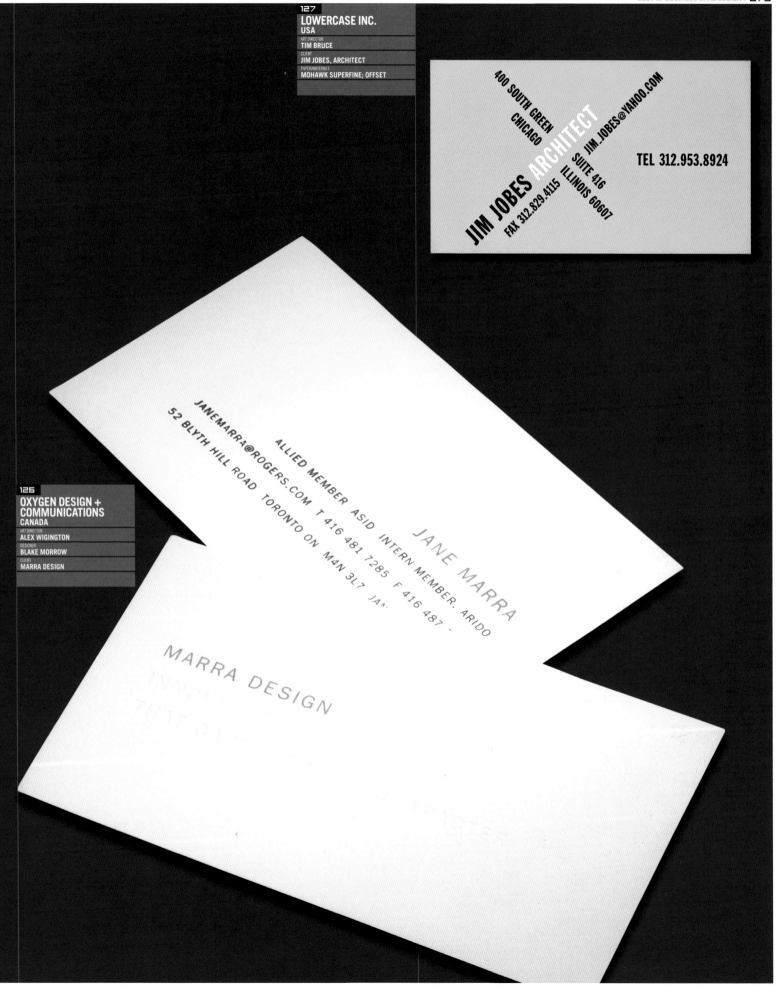

127

LOWERCASE INC.
USA
ART DIRECTOR
TIM BRUCE
CLIENT
JIM JOBES, ARCHITECT
PAPER/MATERIALS
MOHAWK SUPERFINE; OFFSET

400 SOUTH GREEN
CHICAGO
JIM.JOBES@YAHOO.COM
JIM JOBES ARCHITECT
SUITE 416
ILLINOIS 60607
FAX 312.829.4115
TEL 312.953.8924

126

**OXYGEN DESIGN +
COMMUNICATIONS**
CANADA
ART DIRECTOR
ALEX WIGINGTON
DESIGNER
BLAKE MORROW
CLIENT
MARRA DESIGN

ALLIED MEMBER ASID INTERN MEMBER. ARIDO
JANEMARRA@ROGERS.COM T 416 481 7285 F 416 487 -
52 BLYTH HILL ROAD TORONTO ON M4N 3L7 JA

JANE MARRA

MARRA DESIGN

ninety nine percent of inspiration is...

humour is the shortest distance between two people

the knowledge

the knowledge

Ryan Wills design director
ryan@taxistudio.co.uk

93 Princess Victoria Street
Clifton Bristol BS8 4DD

Call   +44 (0)117 9735151
        +44 (0)7976 370998
Fax   +44 (0)117 9735181
Visit   **www.taxistudio.co.uk**

taxi studio ltd

on't let the truth get in the way of a good story

the kno

9MYLES INC

Myles McGuinness
Chief Mechanic

☐ REGULAR ☐ PLUS ☒ PREMIUM

858-344-8619
WWW.9MYLES.COM
FUEL@9MYLES.COM

FUEL FOR THOUGHT.

ow the
pographic
es
before
a
kin'
n

the knowledge

widows
should not
be hyphe-
nated

the knowledge

129
TAXI STUDIO
UNITED KINGDOM
ART DIRECTOR
SPENCER BUCK
DESIGNER
RYAN WILLS
CLIENT
TAXI STUDIO
PAPER/MATERIALS
VERUS ION 300 GSM

130
KESSELSKRAMER
THE NETHERLANDS
ART DIRECTORS
ERIK KESSELS
KRISTA ROZEMA
CLIENT
DO

128
9MYLES, INC.
USA
ART DIRECTOR
MYLES MCGUINNESS
DESIGNER
MYLES MCGUINNESS
CLIENT
9MYLES, INC.
PAPER/MATERIALS
CLASSIC CREST 100# COVER

lauriergracht 39
1016 rg amsterdam
p.o. box 3240
1001 aa amsterdam
the netherlands
phone +31(0)20 5301070
fax +31(0)20 5301061
e-mail domail@dosurf.com
website www.dosurf.com

NTAINS 9M. PROLONGED
EASE YOUR BOTTOM LINE.

SEAN M. KINNEY
GRAPHIC DESIGNER
Cell: 732.221.3519
smkinney@comcast.net

*cutting

DIANNA NILSS

diannanilsson@ti

www.diannanils

Stampesgade 7, 1tv   P: +45 / 4072 1502
DK-1702 Copenhagen V   M: +45 / 4072 1502

131
MUGGIE RAMADANI
DESIGN STUDIO
DENMARK
ART DIRECTOR
MUGGIE RAMADANI
DESIGNER
MUGGIE RAMADANI
CLIENT
DIANNA NILSSON, PHOTOGRAPHER

Stampesgade 7, 1tv
DK-1702 Copenhagen V

DIANNA NILSSON

132
S. M. KINNEY DESIGN
USA

DESIGNER
SEAN M. KINNEY

CLIENT
SELF-PROMOTION

PAPER/MATERIALS
ETCHED STAINLESS STEEL

cutting edge

SEAN M. KINNEY
GRAPHIC DESIGNER
Cell: 732.221.3519
smkinney@comcast.net

133
JAN BARKER AND
DAVID CAUNCE
UNITED KINGDOM

ART DIRECTOR
JAN BARKER

DESIGNERS
JAN BARKER
DAVID CAUNCE

CLIENT
COOGAN & CO.

PAPER/MATERIALS
350 GSM SILK
MATTE LAMINATION

COOGAN & Co.
stunning flowers for sensational events

WENDY MORROW : 07791 478140
35 BURLINGTON ROAD MANCHESTER M20 4QA

DARREN CRITZ Managing Director

138 South Oxford St. Room 5A
Brooklyn, NY 11217
718.398.3095 fax 718.398.3613
darren@TargetMargin.org

LENORE DOXSEE
Production Manager/Resident Designer

138 South Oxford St. Room 5A
Brooklyn, NY 11217
718.398.3095 fax 718.398.3613
Lenore@TargetMargin.org

138 South Oxford St. Room 5A
Brooklyn, NY 11217
718.398.3095 fax 718.398.3613
www.TargetMargin.org

DAVID HERSKOVITS Artistic Director

138 South Oxford St. Room 5A
Brooklyn, NY 11217
718.398.3095 fax 718.398.3613
david@targetmargin.org

134
ALR DESIGN
USA

ART DIRECTOR
NOAH SCALIN

DESIGNER
NOAH SCALIN

CLIENT
TARGET MARGIN THEATER

PAPER/MATERIALS
ROLLAND MOTIF SCREEN

135
BLOK DESIGN
MEXICO

ART DIRECTOR
VANESSA ECKSTEIN

DESIGNER
VANESSA ECKSTEIN

CLIENT
DISTRITO FILMS

PAPER/MATERIALS
STRATHMORE ULTIMATE WHITE

136
804© GRAPHIC DESIGN
GERMANY

ART DIRECTORS
HELGE RIEDER
OLIVER HENN

DESIGNERS
HELGE RIEDER
OLIVER HENN

CLIENT
804© GRAPHIC DESIGN

PAPER/MATERIALS
OFFSET AND SCREENPRINTING
RÖMERTURM COLAMBO
GLETSCHER GLATT

Ó!
Hönnun og auglýsingar
Klapparstíg 16
101 Reykjavík
Sími 562 3300

EINAR GYLFASON
HönnuðurFÍT
840 0220
einar@oid.is
www.oid.is

138
Ó!
ICELAND
ART DIRECTOR
EINAR GYLFASON
DESIGNER
EINAR GYLFASON
CLIENT
Ó!
PAPER/MATERIALS
MUNKEN LYNX

Diane Gasson Executive Assistant
CIRCLE BANK 1400A Grant Avenue, Novato, CA 94945
t {415} 898.5400 f {415} 898.3742 www.circlebank.com

t {415} 493.3101 direct
dgasson@circlebank.com

Circle
BANK

137
MORTENSEN DESIGN INC.
USA
ART DIRECTOR
GORDON MORTENSEN
DESIGNER
ANN JORDAN
CLIENT
CIRCLE BANK
PAPER/MATERIALS
CORONADO

139
ROMEN DESIGN
THE NETHERLANDS

ART DIRECTOR
RAUL RODRIGUEZ
DESIGNER
RAUL RODRIGUEZ
CLIENT
ROMEN DESIGN
PAPER/MATERIALS
TARGET PLUS WHITE 300 GSM

another :: point :: of :: view

ROMENDESIGN

:: RAUL RODRIGUEZ
   Designer

ROMENDESIGN

:: Boergoorn 13 9403 NX Assen
   The Netherlands

:: T +31 592 344 006
   F +31 592 343 118
   M +31 628 554 864
   info@romendesign.nl
   www.romendesign.nl

an emergent property

phonomat

99 Fifth Avenue
Suite no. 249
Ottawa Ontario
K1S 5P5
Canada

facsimile 1.800.475.2724

bureau 1.800.521.2715

intercontinental 1.613.321.7147

phonomat
*the new deal for the
steel wheel !*

Stefan St. Jacques
stefan@phonomat.ca
www.phonomat.ca

140
PHONOMAT
CANADA

ART DIRECTOR
STEFAN ST. JACQUES
DESIGNER
STEFAN ST. JACQUES
CLIENT
SELF-PROMOTION
PAPER/MATERIALS
**12 PT. CORNWALL WITH 2-SIDED
DELUSTRED MATTE LAMINATION**

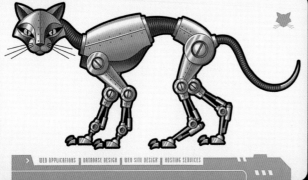

141
GLITSCHKA STUDIOS
USA
ART DIRECTOR
VON R. GLITSCHKA
DESIGNER
VON R. GLITSCHKA
CLIENT
ROBOTICAT COMMUNICATIONS
PAPER/MATERIALS
12 PT. SUPER-PREMIUM KROMEKOTE

142
**CAMPBELL FISHER
DESIGN**
USA
ART DIRECTOR
GREG FISHER
DESIGNERS
**STACY CRAWFORD
KEN PETERS**
CLIENT
ELITE AXIS

141
GLITSCHKA STUDIOS
USA

143

LLOYD'S GRAPHIC DESIGN LTD.
NEW ZEALAND

ART DIRECTOR
ALEXANDER LLOYD

DESIGNER
ALEXANDER LLOYD

CLIENT
VANDERCOUP INTERIOR DESIGN & COLOR CONSULTANT

PAPER/MATERIALS
MATTE UNCOATED BOARD 300 GSM

Hey, wearesoul.....
visit us.

www.wearesoul.co.uk
hey@wearesoul.co.uk

Hey, wearesoul.....
visit us.

www.wearesoul.co.uk
hey@wearesoul.co.uk

Hey, wearesoul.....
visit us.

www.wearesoul.co.uk
hey@wearesoul.co.uk

145
TRANSMUTE
UNITED KINGDOM
DESIGNER
CHRIS MCCLEAN
CLIENT
SOUL
PAPER/MATERIALS
250 GSM UNCOATED BOARD

144
THOMPSON
UNITED KINGDOM
ART DIRECTOR
IAN THOMPSON
DESIGNER
STEVE WILLS
CLIENT
THOMPSON
PAPER/MATERIALS
CONQUEROR DIAMOND WHITE
WOVE 300 GSM

Thompson   **ArticulatingBrandVision**

David Thompson
Designer
Mobile 07816 856765

The Old Stables
Springwood Gardens
Leeds LS8 2QB
Tel +44 (0)113 232 9222
Fax +44 (0)113 232 3775
davidt@thompsondesign.co.uk
www.thompsondesign.co.uk

Thompson   **ArticulatingBrandVision**

Paul Phillips
Senior Designer
Mobile 07717 780639

The Old Stables
Springwood Gardens
Leeds LS8 2QB
Tel +44 (0)113 232 9222
Fax +44 (0)113 232 3775
paul@thompsondesign.co.uk
www.thompsondesign.co.uk

Thompson   **ArticulatingBrandVision**

Liz Calvert
Account Director
Mobile 07710 592428

The Old Stables
Springwood Gardens
Leeds LS8 2QB
Tel +44 (0)113 232 9222
Fax +44 (0)113 232 3775
liz@thompsondesign.co.uk
www.thompsondesign.co.uk

Nicola Stephenson
Artistic Director

Mobile 07970 370 301
nicola@theculturecompany.co.uk

the culture company

Kirklees Media Centre
7 Northumberland Street
Huddersfield HD1 1RL

Tel +44 (0) 1484 483183
Fax +44 (0) 1484 483180
info@theculturecompany.co.uk
www.theculturecompany.co.uk

FIND CULTURE HERE

146
THOMPSON
UNITED KINGDOM

ART DIRECTOR:
IAN THOMPSON

DESIGNER
DAVID THOMPSON

CLIENT
THE CULTURE COMPANY

PAPER/MATERIALS
**CONQUEROR DIAMOND WHITE
WOVE 300 GSM**

H7
**3RD EDGE
COMMUNICATIONS**
USA
ART DIRECTOR
FRANKIE GONZALEZ
DESIGNER
MELISSA MEDINA MACKIN
CLIENT
3RD EDGE COMMUNICATIONS

FRANKIE GONZALEZ
president

162 NEWARK AVENUE
3RD FLOOR
JERSEY CITY, NJ 07302
P 201.395.9960
F 201.395.0044
E FRANKIE@3RDEDGE.COM

WWW.3RDEDGE.COM

Moda Design Group Pty Ltd PO B

150
OCTAVO
AUSTRALIA
ART DIRECTOR
GARY DOMONEY
CLIENT
KEY FINANCIAL GROUP
PAPER/MATERIALS
**360 GSM WHITE A ARTBOARD
MATTE FILM LAMINATION; FOIL STAMP**

key financial group

key financial group pty ltd 187 ferrars street southbank 3006 victoria
telephone: 03 9696 4411 facsimile: 03 9696 4611 mobile: 0410 568 539
email: grant@keyfinancial.com.au website: www.keyfinancial.com.au

grant matthews managing director

moda

148
OCTAVO
AUSTRALIA
ART DIRECTOR
GARY DOMONEY
CLIENT
MODA DESIGN GROUP
PAPER/MATERIALS
**360 GSM WHITE A ARTBOARD
MATTE FILM LAMINATION**

T
F
M
E
W

03 8598 9333
03 8598 9344
0411 569 039
as@modadesign.com.au
www.modadesign.com.au
St Kilda 3182 Victoria Australia

Angelo Sansano Director

149
FUNNEL
USA
DESIGNER
ERIC KASS
CLIENT
DAVE HEPLER
PAPER/MATERIALS
**FRENCH; CONSTRUCTION
CHARCOAL BROWN 100# COVER**

Dave Hepler 317 255 3893

(Pianist)

7029 North Central Avenue
Indianapolis Indiana United States of America 46220
davehepler.com

Stéphane Husar DIRECTOR
PO BOX 561, WOOLLAHRA NSW 1350, AUSTRALIA
PHONE 61-2-9699 6466 MOB 0403 766 441
STEF@SOUNDREPUBLIC.COM.AU
SOUNDREPUBLIC.COM.AU

151

BOCCALATTE
AUSTRALIA
ART DIRECTOR
SUZANNE BOCCALATTE
DESIGNER
SUZANNE BOCCALATTE
CLIENT
STEPHANE MUSAR – SOUND REPUBLIC
PAPER/MATERIALS
352 GSM EXPRESSION; UNCOATED

NAME: **Raphael Pohland** Dipl. Designer (FH)

EMAIL: pohland@stilradar.de

stilradar visual resources   Schwabstr. 10a   70197 Stuttgart

T 0711 887 55 20   F 0711 882 23 44   M 0172 735 45 21

www.stilradar.de

152

STILRADAR
GERMANY
ART DIRECTORS
RAPHAEL POHLAND
SIMONE WINTER
CLIENT
STILRADAR

the sanctuary

STEPHANIE PERRONE
Spa Director

T. 415.901.9312
F. 415.433.7161
E. sperrone@sfbayclub.com
A. 150 Greenwich Street, San Francisco, CA 94111

153
BUCHANAN DESIGN
USA
ART DIRECTOR
BOBBY BUCHANAN
DESIGNERS
DARYLL PIERCE
HOLLY JONES
CLIENT
THE SAN FRANCISCO BAY CLUB
PAPER/MATERIALS
NEENAH CLASSIC CREST
NATURAL WHITE; 80# COVER

Jon loves yoghurt.

Jon loves sparkling water.

Luc Dahlhaus

André Olyslager

Postbus 1546. 1000 BM Amsterdam
Phone 020-4275358. www.jon-n-jon.com

Postbus 1546. 1000 BM Amsterdam
Phone 020-4275358. www.jon-n-jon.com

154
KESSELSKRAMER
THE NETHERLANDS
ART DIRECTOR
KAREN HEUTER
CLIENT
JON & JON

155

IMAGINE
UNITED KINGDOM

ART DIRECTOR
DAVID CAUNCE

DESIGNER
DAVID CAUNCE

CLIENT
LOOMLAND SILKSCREEN PRINTER

PAPER/MATERIALS
CONQUEROR CX22

156

9MYLES, INC.
USA

ART DIRECTOR
MYLES MCGUINNESS

DESIGNER
MYLES MCGUINNESS

CLIENT
IDENTITYWEAR STUDIOS

PAPER/MATERIALS
CHIPBOARD; 120# COVER

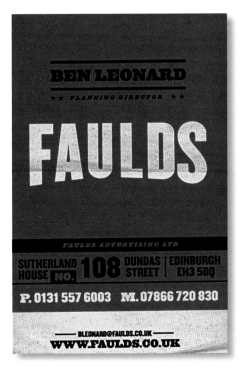

157

UNREAL
UNITED KINGDOM

ART DIRECTOR
BRIAN EAGLE

DESIGNER
BRIAN EAGLE

CLIENT
FAULDS (ADVERTISING AGENCY)

158

SPACEDUST DESIGN
USA

DESIGNER
PATRICK SULLIVAN

CLIENT
PATRICK SULLIVAN

PAPER/MATERIALS
3-COLOR SCREEN PRINT ON CHIPBOARD

159
PENSARÉ DESIGN GROUP LTD.
USA
ART DIRECTOR
MARY ELLEN VEHLOW
DESIGNER
KUNDIA WOOD
CLIENT
CUPPA' JO COFFEE HOUSE
PAPER/MATERIALS
UNCOATED 2-COLOR

160
MICHAEL THIELE
GERMANY
DESIGNER
MICHAEL THIELE
CLIENT
EDWARDS
PAPER/MATERIALS
230 GSM MATTE; COATED

161
LOWERCASE INC.
USA
ART DIRECTOR
TIM BRUCE
CLIENT
RICHARD E. SMITH
PAPER/MATERIALS
MOHAWK SUPERFINE, LETTERPRESS

162
HAND MADE SRL
ITALY
ART DIRECTOR
ALESSANDRO ESTERI
DESIGNER
ALESSANDRO ESTERI
CLIENT
PODERE BELVEDERE ORGANIC FARM

163
PHASE05
USA
ART DIRECTORS
LINDA LOIEWSKI
TERRY LUSH
DESIGNERS
LINDA LOIEWSKI
TERRY LUSH
CLIENT
PHASE05
PAPER/MATERIALS
TOUCHÉ® COVER

phase05
creative union

AL PENTA
24 WEST MAIN ST. 105 CLINTON, CT 06413-2090
APENTA@PHASE05.COM
LANDLINE: 860 669 8675
MOBILE: 203 376 3471

www.phase05.com

THIAGO BARROS
FOTOGRAFIA
LABORATÓRIO PB
21 2502 5292
21 9189 8065
thiago@
thiagobarros.com

164
V06
BRAZIL
ART DIRECTOR
YOMAR AUGUSTO
DESIGNER
YOMAR AUGUSTO
CLIENT
THIAGO BARROS
PAPER/MATERIALS
COLOR PLUS / BLACK

165
CIRCLE K STUDIO
USA

ART DIRECTOR
JULIE KEENAN
DESIGNER
JULIE KEENAN
CLIENT
JACK GESCHEIDT
PAPER/MATERIALS
CENTURA SILK 130# COVER

Jack Gescheidt *photographer*
4340 Anza Street #7 San Francisco California 94121
tel & fax 415 668 5225   jack@jackphoto.com
www.jackphoto.com

kellhofer

unreal

166
UNREAL
UNITED KINGDOM

ART DIRECTOR
BRIAN EAGLE
DESIGNER
BRIAN EAGLE
CLIENT
UNREAL

unreal-u
brian.eagle
020 7379

666 High Street
Palo Alto, CA 94301
Voice: 650.327.0707
Fax: 650.327.0699
sam@samsmidt.com
www.samsmidt.com

Sam Smidt

167
SAM SMIDT
USA
DESIGNER
SAM SMIDT
CLIENT
SAM SMIDT
PAPER/MATERIALS
130# STARWHITE

168
CIRCLE K STUDIO
USA
ART DIRECTOR
JULIE KEENAN
DESIGNER
JULIE KEENAN
CLIENT
MODA-MIA, INC.
PAPER/MATERIALS
**STARWHITE VICKSBURG
TIARA WHITE, 130# COVER**

Peter Ricci,   Director, Business Development

Moda-Mia, A 7x7, Inc. Company
530 Divisadero Street, Suite 327
San Francisco, CA 94117-2213
tel 888-MODA-MIA   fax 415-276-8931
peter@moda-mia.com   www.moda-mia.com

moda-mia

JOINT

JOINT

Peter Wiedensmith
317 SW Alder, S
Port

JOINT

Peter Wiedensmith
317 SW Alder, Suite 507
Portland, OR 97204
503.525.4630
Fax 503.525.4633

(P) 812 339 3039
(F) 812 333 2278
(W) fifth street net

5

2

fifthstreet
DESIGN/PRINT/WEB

1018 fifth street n
minneapolis mn
55411 usa

(A)

170
PLAZM
USA
ART DIRECTOR
NIKO COURTELIS
DESIGNER
NIKO COURTELIS
CLIENT
JOINT
PRINTING
CRACK PRESS
PAPER/MATERIALS
ONION SKIN PAPER

169
FIFTH STREET DESIGN
USA
ART DIRECTOR
DAN WEST
DESIGNERS
DAN WEST
DANN VOORHEES
CLIENT
FIFTH STREET DESIGN
PAPER/MATERIALS
FOX RIVER TIARA WHITE
LETTERPRESS; DIE CUT

171
**ENTERMOTION
DESIGN STUDIO**
USA
ART DIRECTORS
**BRIAN CARTWRIGHT
JOE MORROW**
DESIGNER
LEA CARMICHAEL
CLIENT
MARSHMALLOW KISSES
PAPER/MATERIALS
COUGAR OPAQUE SMOOTH

AVEC AMIS

SERENA ARMSTRONG

EVENT PLANNING & STYLING
206.324.2552 | SERENA@AVECAMIS.COM
AVECAMIS.COM

172
WOLKEN COMMUNICA
USA
ART DIRECTOR
KURT WOLKEN
DESIGNER
JULIE SCHNEIDER
CLIENT
AVEC AMIS

620 North Delaware Street / Suite 100 / Indianapolis Indiana 46204

TELEPHONE
: 317 631 3003 :

FACSIMILE
: 317 631 0460 :

Harold Lee Miller

HAROLD LEE MILLER

Photographer

HAROLDLEEMILLER.COM

173

LODGE DESIGN CO.
USA
DESIGNER
ERIC KASS
CLIENT
HAROLD LEE MILLER, PHOTOGRAPHER
PAPER/MATERIALS
100# WHITE COVER

174

> PROMPTT
USA
ART DIRECTOR
CORRINE MORITA
DESIGNER
CORRINE MORITA
CLIENT
> PROMPTT
PAPER/MATERIALS
CRANE 100% COTTON 110#

IO SERIES

Tag No.
94107

> PROMPTT   [415 431 4173]

> PROMPTT

name:
GEORGE ARRIOLA
location:
49 MISSOURI STREET NO.IO

SAN FRANCISCO CA 94107
part no.   mobile no.
                            415 309 3108
aim:
brandexperience
email: date:
george@promptt.com

Enter only one item on tag.
All tags must be accounted for.   Tag No.
                                          94107

IO SERIES

Tag No.
94107

> PROMPTT   [415 431 4173]

promptt

name:
CORRINE M MORITA
location:
49 MISSOURI STREET NO.IO

SAN FRANCISCO CA 94107
part no.   Phone no.
                            415 431 4173
email: date:
corrine@promptt.com

Enter only one item on tag. All tags must be accounted for.

Tag No. 94107

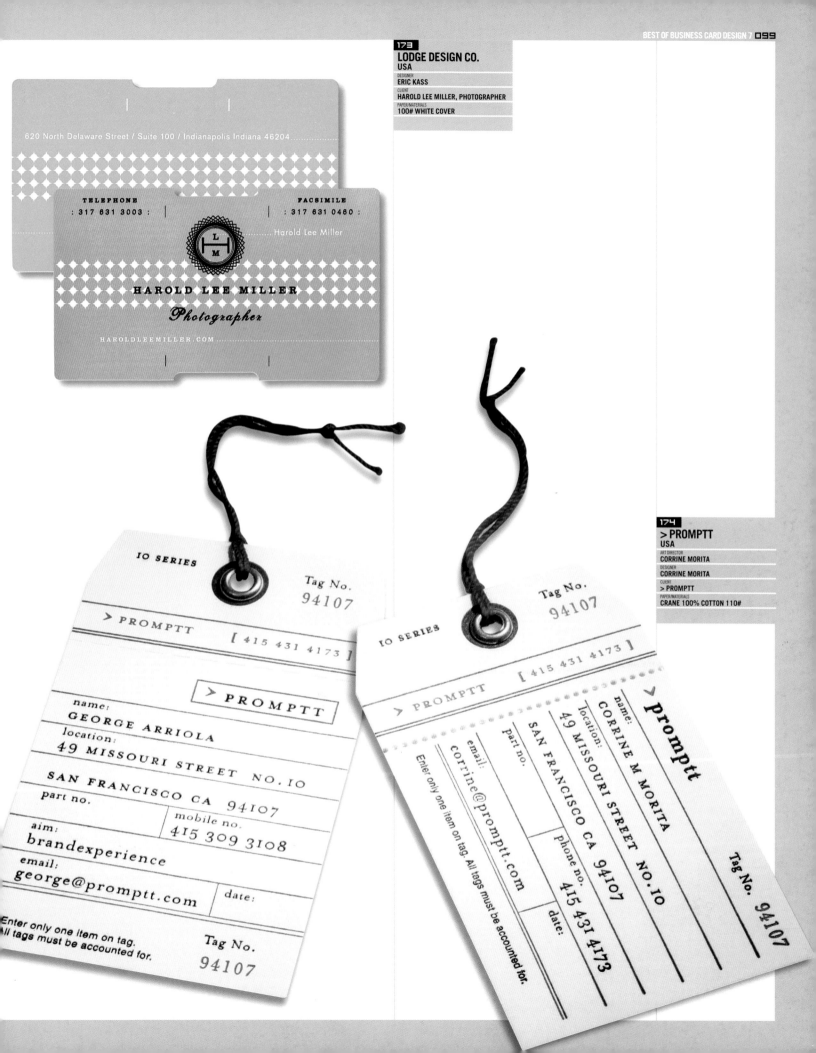

175

GRAPHISCHE FORMGEBUNG
GERMANY

ART DIRECTOR
HERBERT ROHSIEPE

DESIGNER
HERBERT ROHSIEPE

CLIENT
ALEXANDER PABLO STEINGASS

PAPER/MATERIALS
ARJO WIGGINS IMPRESSIONS RIVES ARTIST SENSATIONS

Katernberger Schulweg 136
42113 Wuppertal

T 02 02.7 67 01 65
F 02 02.7 67 02 99
M 01 73.5 46 86 80
E pablissimo@gmx.de

alexander pablo ● steingass

176

SLANT, INC.
USA

ART DIRECTORS
**RYAN GAGNARD
DAVID SLACK**

DESIGNER
RYAN GAGNARD

CLIENT
W2

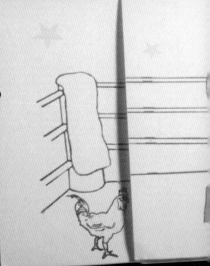

W2   Plan / Design / Build

W2 STUDIO

W2

7045 Clayton Avenue   214-328-2448 **tel**
Dallas, Texas 75214   214-324-3142 **fax**

Melissa Williams, AAIA
melissa@w2studio.com

brian eagle

07787 572103 · · · · · · · · · · · · DESIGN DIRECTOR

brian.eagle@unreal-uk.com · · · · · · · · · ·

TEL 020 7379 8752
FAX 020 7379 7380
ISDN 020 7379 8858

www.unreal-uk.com

2-4 bucknall street
london WC2H 8LA

unreal

EST. 1995

UNREST

UN BEATEN

178
KINETIC SINGAPORE
SINGAPORE
ART DIRECTOR
ROY POH
DESIGNER
ROY POH
CLIENT
ART DOMINUS
PAPER/MATERIALS
SILKWIND WHITE 280 GSM

177
UNREAL
UNITED KINGDOM
ART DIRECTOR
BRIAN EAGLE
DESIGNER
BRIAN EAGLE
CLIENT
UNREAL

ad

art dominus

Zach Fahy
Managing Director

128H Carnhill Road
Singapore 229716
M. 9178 1729
E. zachfahy@hotmail.com

179

BLOK DESIGN
MEXICO
ART DIRECTOR
VANESSA ECKSTEIN
DESIGNERS
VANESSA ECKSTEIN
FRANCES CHEN
CLIENT
EL ZANJON
PAPER/MATERIALS
STRATHMORE ULTIMATE WHITE

180

32BITS™ DESIGN
EM MULTIMEIOS
BRAZIL
DESIGNERS
DANIEL MORENA
NEI CARAMÊS
CLIENT
32BITS™ DESIGN EM MULTIMEIOS
PAPER/MATERIALS
4-COLOR PRINT ON OPTICAL
LENTICULAR PAPER

Stephanie Wurm

ZEHLENDORFER WEG 6 ✦ 44388 DORTMUND
TELEFON 0321/6181042 ✦ MOBILFON 0177/3642264
STEPHIE.WURM@WEB.DE

181
**WERBE- &
MEDIEN-AKADEMIE
MARQUARDT—
CARINA BUSMANN**
GERMANY
ART DIRECTOR
MARTIN SCHONHOFF
DESIGNER
CARINA BUSMANN
CLIENT
STEPHANIE WURM
PAPER/MATERIALS
160 GSM; BEIGE
NATURAL STRUCTURE

182
**METAMARK
INTERNATIONAL LTD.**
ISRAEL
ART DIRECTORS
DORON DEKEL
YANEK IONTEF
DESIGNER
YANEK IONTEF
CLIENT
METAMARK INTERNATIONAL LTD.
PAPER/MATERIALS
OFFSET PRINTING ON COATED PAPER

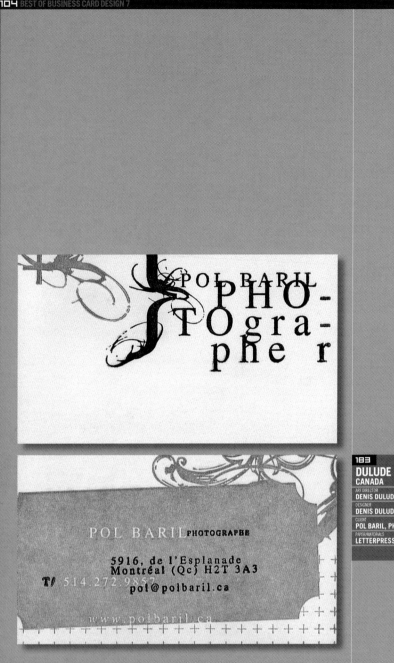

Kathryn.

+44 7990 521 642
kathryn@kathrynmccusker.com

www.anjalisisters.com
www.xiexietea.com

POL BARIL
PHO-
TOgra-
pher

POL BARIL PHOTOGRAPHE

5916, de l'Esplanade
Montréal (Qc) H2T 3A3
T/ 514.272.9857
pol@polbaril.ca

www.polbaril.ca

184

ALOOF DESIGN
UNITED KINGDOM

ART DIRECTOR
SAM ALOOF

DESIGNER
ANDREW SCRASE

CLIENT
KATHRYN MCCUSKER

PAPER/MATERIALS
STOCK T6C

183

DULUDE
CANADA

ART DIRECTOR
DENIS DULUDE

DESIGNER
DENIS DULUDE

CLIENT
POL BARIL, PHOTOGRAPHER

PAPER/MATERIALS
LETTERPRESS

185

TRIANA THE
USA

DESIGNER
TRIANA THE

CLIENT
CATRINE THE

PAPER/MATERIALS
STOCK CARD

---

catrine_the@hotmail.com 917.573.2885

fashion illustrator ♥

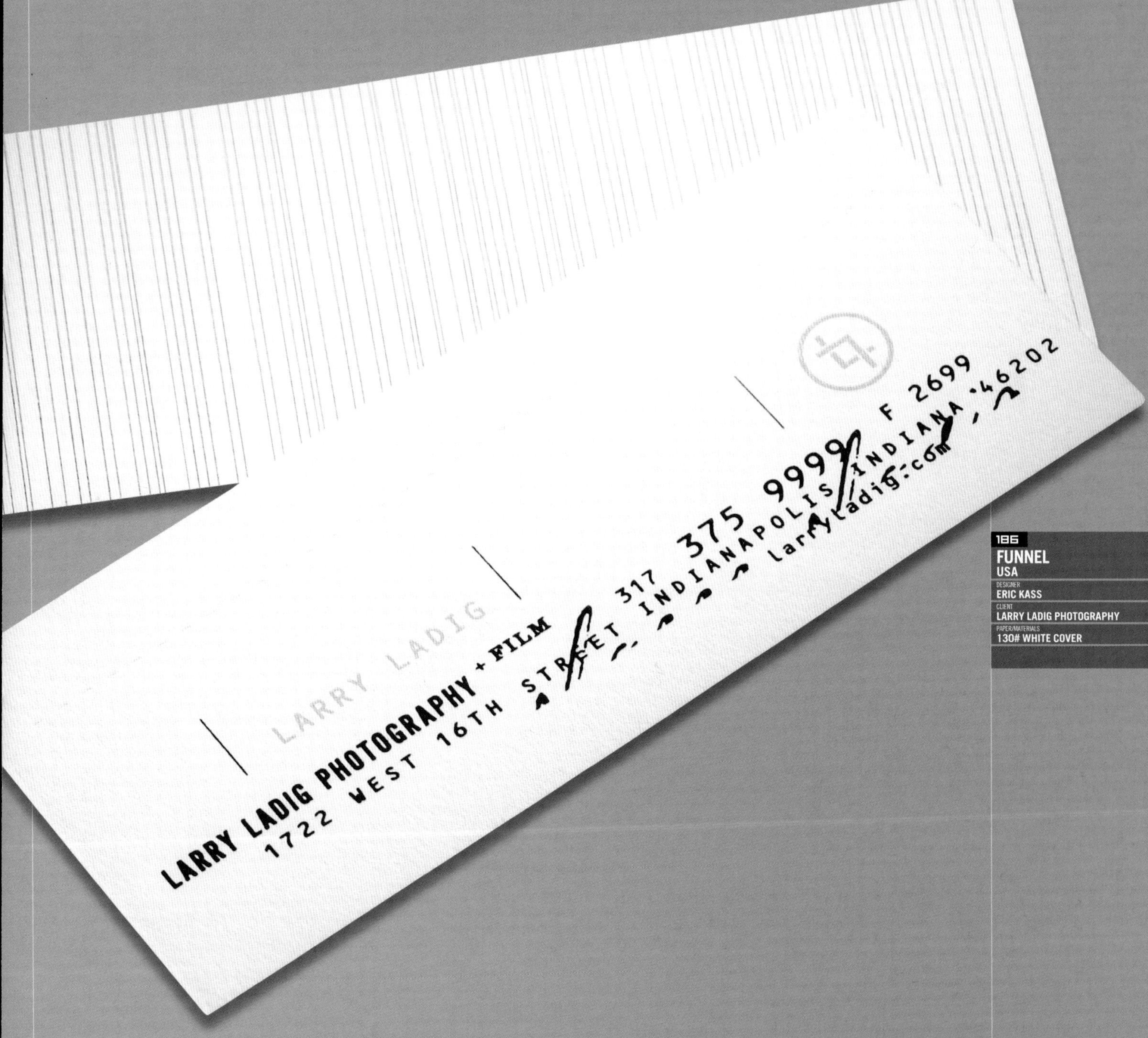

LARRY LADIG

LARRY LADIG PHOTOGRAPHY + FILM
1722 WEST 16TH STREET 317 375 9999 F 2699
INDIANAPOLIS INDIANA 46202
larryladig:com

186
FUNNEL
USA
DESIGNER
ERIC KASS
CLIENT
LARRY LADIG PHOTOGRAPHY
PAPER/MATERIALS
130# WHITE COVER

MC**CORMACK**SPORTSINC.
BERGMANNSTR. 22 44145 DORTMUND
FON///+49 28 41.8 80 84 84 FAX///+49 28 41.8 80 84 87
WWW.MC-SPORTS.**COM**

187

**WERBE- &
MEDIEN-AKADEMIE
MARQUARDT—
ANDRE MEDGER**
GERMANY

ART DIRECTOR
MARTIN SCHONHOFF
DESIGNER
ANDRE MEDGER
CLIENT
MCCORMACK SPORTS INC.
PAPER/MATERIALS
230 GSM WHITE MATTE

188

WING CHAN DESIGN
USA

ART DIRECTOR
WING CHAN
DESIGNER
WING CHAN
CLIENT
WING CHAN DESIGN
PAPER/MATERIALS
BECKETT EXPRESSION RADIANCE

167 Perry Street 5C   T 212 727 9109   wingchandesign.ny@verizon.net
New York NY 10014   F 212 727 8742   www.wingchandesign.com

WingChanDesignInc.

167 Perry Street, 5C   tel 212-727-9109   wing@wingchandesign.com
New York, NY 10014   fax 212-727-8742   www.wingchandesign.com

WingChanDesignInc.

make life simple.™

3910 Pecan Drive
Alexandria, LA 71302
Tel 318.442.0384
Fax 318.448.0441
ideas@voilahh.com

VOILA

www.exposoft.com

2145 MEADOWPINE BLVD.
MISSISSAUGA, ON L5N 6R8

1.888.304.9161

T 905.812.3770
F 905.812.3714

189
FRANK FORD
USA
DESIGNER
FRANK FORD
CLIENT
VOILA
PAPER/MATERIALS
YUPO

190
**SPLASH
INTERACTIVE LTD.**
CANADA
ART DIRECTOR
IVY WONG
DESIGNERS
**IVY WONG
MARCOS ERIN**
CLIENT
EXPOSOFT SOLUTIONS
PAPER/MATERIALS
**EUROSILK
DEBOSS
FOIL**

teddy lo
creative director
SLAVE DRIVER
cell 917.208.7872
office 212.925.1330
437 EAST 18th STREET
UNIT south 27J
NEW YORK
NY 10016
teddylo@ledartist.com

demiurge
unit

192
DEMIURGE UNIT
USA
ART DIRECTOR
TEDDY LO
DESIGNER
TRIANA THE
CLIENT
DEMIURGE UNIT

191
WERBE- &
MEDIEN-AKADEMIE
MARQUARDT—
KAROLIN BUSCH
GERMANY
ART DIRECTOR
MARTIN SCHONHOFF
DESIGNER
KAROLIN BUSCH
CLIENT
MEIKE HOLLERBUHL
PAPER/MATERIALS
200 GSM PAPER

Flurstraße 74 | Meike Hollerbuhl | 44145 Dortmund
+49.2 31.33 67 19 | +49.1 62.6 15 96 28
m.hollerbuhl@arcor.de

**THOMAS
KARCZEWSKI**
FRIEDRICH-EBERT-STRASSE 11A
59425 Unna

TELEFON (0 23 03) 25 77 75
FAX (0 23 03) 25 77 76
MOBIL (0179) 7 34 08 77
THOKA@GMX.NET

194
**WERBE- &
MEDIEN-AKADEMIE
MARQUARDT—
INGO DRECKMANN**
GERMANY
ART DIRECTOR
MARTIN SCHONHOFF
DESIGNER
INGO DRECKMANN
CLIENT
THOMAS KARCZEWSKI
PAPER/MATERIALS
150 GSM WHITE

K O O N
·
lkoonhor@ya
917.774.9

K O O N
·
917.774.9789
oonhor@yahoo.com

193
TRIANA THE
USA
DESIGNER
TRIANA THE
CLIENT
KOON
PAPER/MATERIALS
**NEEDLE
THREAD
CARDSTOCK**

{ **350** MOUNT PLEASANT RD TORONTO ONTARIO M4T 2C8 }

tel +416 932 1013 › surkl@rogers.com

{ **350** MOUNT PLEASANT RD TORONTO ONTARIO M4T 2C8 }

tel +416 932 1013 › surkl@rogers.com

{ **350** MOUNT PLEASANT RD TORONTO ONTARIO M4T 2C8 }

tel +416 932 1013 › surkl@rogers.com

195
BLOK DESIGN
MEXICO

ART DIRECTOR
VANESSA ECKSTEIN

DESIGNERS
VANESSA ECKSTEIN
VANESSA ENRIQUEZ

CLIENT
SÛRKL

PAPER/MATERIALS
FOX RIVER
SIRIUS SMOOTH

bungee associates

Joe Tjiam
creative consultant
hp 9755 2211

www.bungeeassociates.com

bungee associates

bungee associates

Lee Wai Leng
creative consultant
hp. 9863 4015

MELANIE LENZ

197
Q
GERMANY
ART DIRECTOR
MARCEL KUMMERER
DESIGNER
MARCEL KUMMERER
CLIENT
MELANIE LENZ

melanie lenz_diplom-designer
pappelallee 8_10437 berlin_telefon 0 30 41 72 59 58_mobil 01 63 4 28 30 93
mail@melanielenz.de_www.melanielenz.de

196
BUNGEE ASSOCIATES
SINGAPORE
ART DIRECTORS
JOE TJIAM
GWEN NG
LEE WAI LENG
DESIGNERS
JOE TJIAM
GWEN NG
LEE WAI LENG
CLIENT
BUNGEE ASSOCIATES
PAPER/MATERIALS
250 GSM MATTE ART CARD

198
ELFEN
UNITED KINGDOM
DESIGNER
ELFEN
CLIENT
ELFEN
PAPER/MATERIALS
CYCLUS OFFSET

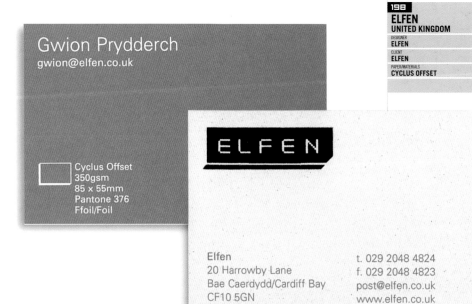

Gwion Prydderch
gwion@elfen.co.uk

Cyclus Offset
350gsm
85 x 55mm
Pantone 376
Ffoil/Foil

ELFEN

Elfen   t. 029 2048 4824
20 Harrowby Lane   f. 029 2048 4823
Bae Caerdydd/Cardiff Bay   post@elfen.co.uk
CF10 5GN   www.elfen.co.uk

SIBLEY PETEET
DESIGN—DALLAS
USA
DESIGNER
BRANDON KIRK
CLIENT
ERIK GOEN
PAPER/MATERIALS
WHITE-COATED HOUSE COVER STOCK

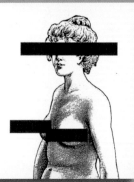

phone: 940.891.6073
email: gauntlette@aol.com

Cut to the b...
through the
it were on r
morphs into
smoothly ove
defined jaw

We now
to see
like tr
close u

Presse le pas petit f@cteur
fabrice.praeger@wanadoo.fr

Fabrice Praeger, 54
bis rue de l'Ermitage,
Paris 75020. Tél : 01 40
33 17 00. Fax : pareil.

200
FABRICE PRAEGER
FRANCE
ART DIRECTOR
FABRICE PRAEGER
DESIGNER
FABRICE PRAEGER
CLIENT
FABRICE PRAEGER
PAPER/MATERIALS
COATED

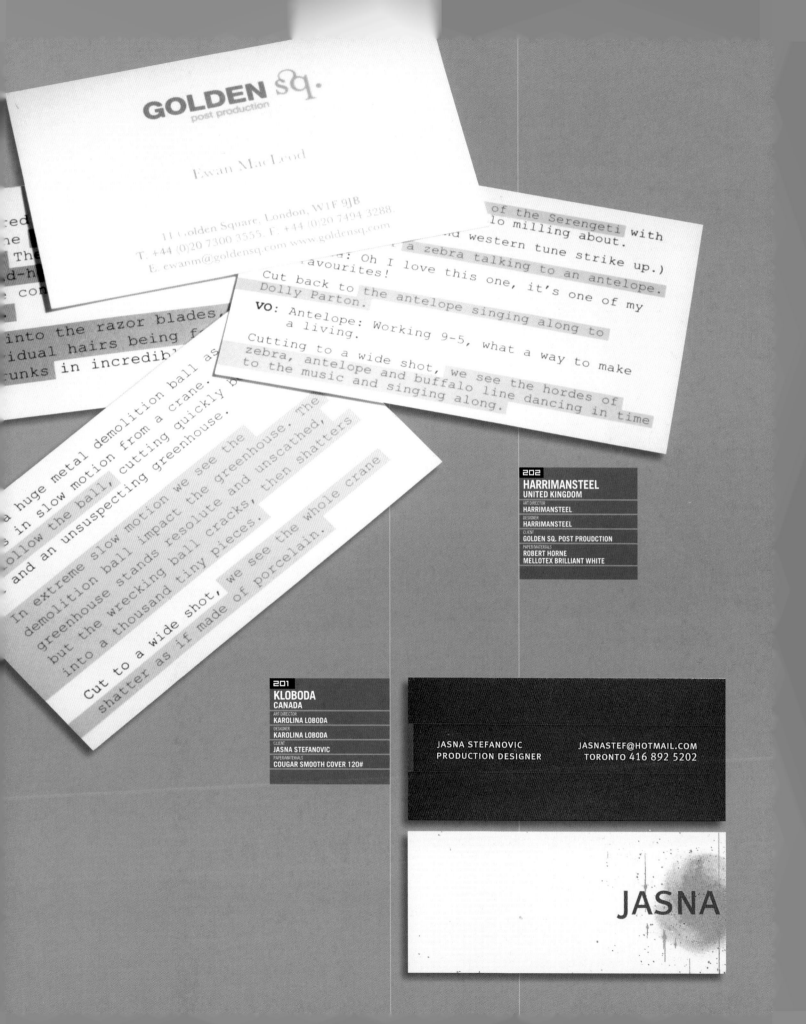

GOLDEN sq.
post production

Ewan MacLeod

11 Golden Square, London, W1F 9JB
T. +44 (0)20 7300 3555. F. +44 (0)20 7494 3288.
E. ewanm@goldensq.com www.goldensq.com

...of the Serengeti with
...lo milling about.
...d western tune strike up.)
...a zebra talking to an antelope.
...favourites!

...ed
...he
The...
d-h...
...con...

...avourites! Oh I love this one, it's one of my
Dolly Parton.

...into the razor blades,...
...idual hairs being f...
...unks in incredibl...

Cut back to the antelope singing along to

VO: Antelope: Working 9-5, what a way to make
a living.

Cutting to a wide shot, we see the hordes of
zebra, antelope and buffalo line dancing in time
to the music and singing along.

...a huge metal demolition ball as...
...s in slow motion from a crane....
...follow the ball, cutting quickly b...
...and an unsuspecting greenhouse.

In extreme slow motion we see the...
demolition ball impact the greenhouse. The...
greenhouse stands resolute and unscathed,...
but the wrecking ball cracks, then shatters...
into a thousand tiny pieces.

Cut to a wide shot, we see the whole crane...
shatter as if made of porcelain.

202
HARRIMANSTEEL
UNITED KINGDOM
ART DIRECTOR
HARRIMANSTEEL
DESIGNER
HARRIMANSTEEL
CLIENT
GOLDEN SQ. POST PROUDCTION
PAPER/MATERIALS
ROBERT HORNE
MELLOTEX BRILLIANT WHITE

201
KLOBODA
CANADA
ART DIRECTOR
KAROLINA LOBODA
DESIGNER
KAROLINA LOBODA
CLIENT
JASNA STEFANOVIC
PAPER/MATERIALS
COUGAR SMOOTH COVER 120#

JASNA STEFANOVIC   JASNASTEF@HOTMAIL.COM
PRODUCTION DESIGNER   TORONTO 416 892 5202

JASNA

GiRASOLE

daniela vitali
designer

400 broome stre
suite 403
new york, ny 1001
phone: 212 343 30
email: daniela@girasolede
www.girasoledesigns

203
GIRASOLE
USA
DESIGNER
DANIELA VITALI
CLIENT
SELF PROMOTION
PAPER/MATERIALS
1-COLOR LETTERPRESS

590×5355

204
FUNNEL
USA
DESIGNER
ERIC KASS
CLIENT
FUNNEL
PAPER/MATERIALS
100# WHITE COVER

SO HONEST IT HURTS

Eric Kass : Utilitarian + Commercial + Fine : Art
Indianapolis Indiana United States of America
***Telephone 317 8180463

www.funnel.tv

FUNNEL

205
EGGERS + DIAPER
GERMANY
ART DIRECTOR
BIRGIT EGGERS
DESIGNER
BIRGIT EGGERS
CLIENT
ANGAR JABIT FASHION DESIGNERS

Anja Ehlers

Hebbelstraße 15

22085 Hamburg

tel   040 - 227 16 747

fax 040 - 227 39 579

Shop & Showroom

tel   040 - 227 39 580

Garbit Ipsen

Hebbelstraße 15

22085 Hamburg

tel   040 - 227 16 747

fax 040 - 227 39 579

Shop & Showroom

tel   040 - 227 39 580

206
A3 DESIGN
USA
ART DIRECTOR
ALAN ALTMAN
DESIGNER
AMANDA ALTMAN
CLIENT
A3 DESIGN
PAPER/MATERIALS
VARIOUS

Seed Intellectual Property Law Group PLLC

Seed IP

Jennifer L. Scully
Attorney at Law
jennifers@SeedIP.com
206.694.4855

address 701 Fifth Avenue
Suite 6300
Seattle, WA 98104
telephone 206.622.4900
facsimile 206.682.6031
website SeedIP.com

207
HORNALL ANDERSON
DESIGN WORKS
USA

ART DIRECTORS
JACK ANDERSON
KATHA DALTON

DESIGNERS
JACK ANDERSON
KATHA DALTON
HENRY YIU
DON STAYNER

CLIENT
SEED INTELLECTUAL PROPERTY
LAW GROUP (SEED IP)

PAPER/MATERIALS
CRANE'S CREST

sweet pea gourmet

Leslie Owen
personal chef

1005 Lindridge Dr. NE
Atlanta, GA 30324

E leslie@sweetpeagourmet.com
P 404.232.5663 F 404.816.1411

208
SKY DESIGN
USA

ART DIRECTOR
W. TODD VAUGHT

DESIGNER
W. TODD VAUGHT

CLIENT
SWEET PEA GOURMET

PAPER/MATERIALS
COUGAR OPAQUE

209
TRIANA THE
USA
DESIGNER
TRIANA THE
CLIENT
YUNIKA KADARUSMAN

YUNIKA KADARUSMAN
photographer

626 821 9214

210
SUM DESIGN
UNITED KINGDOM
ART DIRECTOR
CAMERON LEADBETTER
DESIGNER
CAMERON LEADBETTER
CLIENT
SUM DESIGN
PAPER/MATERIALS
**STRATHMORE ELEMENTS
SILVER FOIL**

118

211

IMAGINE
UNITED KINGDOM

ART DIRECTOR
DAVID CAUNCE

DESIGNER
DAVID CAUNCE

CLIENT
ANTHEM PRODUCTIONS

PAPER/MATERIALS
CONQUEROR CX22

anthem

SIMON MAYO

ANTHEM PRODUCTIONS LIMITED

7 WORSLEY MILL 10 BLANTYRE STREET CASTLEFIELD MANCHESTER M15 4LG
TELEPHONE **0161 827 1632** MOBILE **07900 194120** FACSIMILE **0161 832 9995**
EMAIL **info@anthem.tv** WEB **www.anthem.tv**

Mission - NetChemistry uses its comprehensive knowledge and specialized expertise to streamline the creation of complex solutions accelerating the fusion of technology and forward thinking in the financial services sector.

NETCHEMISTRY

○ Solid | ○ Liquid | ○ Gas

19800 Mac Arthur Blvd, Suite 200 | LEVEL
Irvine, CA 92612 | 949.608.1712
netchemistry.com | 949.608.1701
astamires@netchemistry.com

N° 341

□ 1 □ 2 □ 3 □ 4 □ 5 □ 6 □ 7 □ 8 □ 9 □ 10

Alex Stamires
Partner, Treasury Systems

212

9MYLES, INC.
USA

ART DIRECTOR
MYLES MCGUINNESS

DESIGNER
MYLES MCGUINNESS

CLIENT
NETCHEMISTRY

PAPER/MATERIALS
MOHAWK BRIGHT WHITE; 120# COVER

213
REDBEAN
USA

ART DIRECTOR
MELISSA CROWLEY

DESIGNER
MELISSA CROWLEY

CLIENT
LUCKY DEVIL SOUND

PAPER/MATERIALS
MOHAWK SUPERFINE SOFTWHITE COVER

Dave Pellicciaro

★ ★ ★

LUCKY DEVIL SOUND

www.luckydevilsound.com | dave@luckydevilsound.com

★ ★ ★

415 482 8702

Andrew Bawidamann | Pinup | Design

andrew@bawidamann.com
www.bawidamann.com

214
BAWIDAMANN DESIGN INC.
USA

ART DIRECTOR
ANDREW BAWIDAMANN

DESIGNER
ANDREW BAWIDAMANN

CLIENT
ANDREW BAWIDAMANN

215

ME, ME
USA

ART DIRECTOR
FIEL VALDEZ

DESIGNER
FIEL VALDEZ

CLIENT
LOVELYBRAND

216

**MUGGIE RAMADANI
DESIGN STUDIO**
DENMARK

ART DIRECTOR
MUGGIE RAMADANI

DESIGNER
MUGGIE RAMADANI

CLIENT
PETER KRASILNIKIOFF, PHOTOGRAPHER

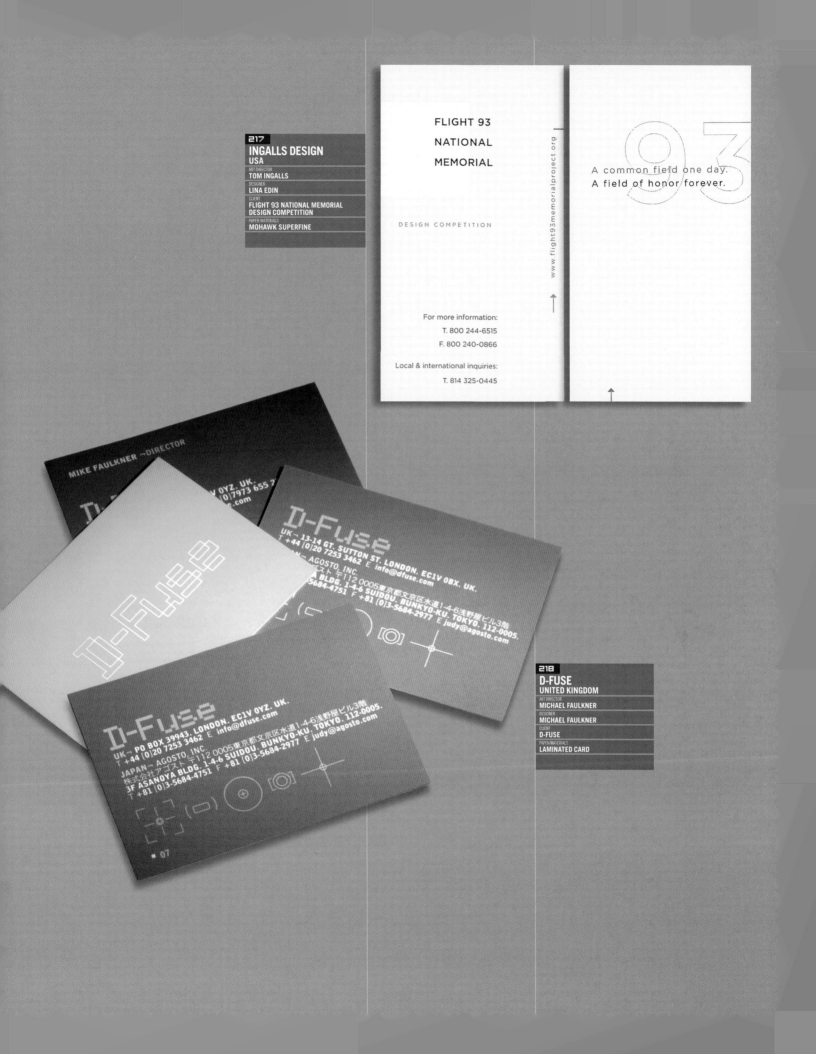

217

INGALLS DESIGN
USA
ART DIRECTOR
TOM INGALLS
DESIGNER
LINA EDIN
CLIENT
FLIGHT 93 NATIONAL MEMORIAL DESIGN COMPETITION
PAPER/MATERIALS
MOHAWK SUPERFINE

FLIGHT 93

NATIONAL

MEMORIAL

DESIGN COMPETITION

For more information:

T. 800 244-6515

F. 800 240-0866

Local & international inquiries:

T. 814 325-0445

www.flight93memorialproject.org

A common field one day.
A field of honor forever.

93

218

D-FUSE
UNITED KINGDOM
ART DIRECTOR
MICHAEL FAULKNER
DESIGNER
MICHAEL FAULKNER
CLIENT
D-FUSE
PAPER/MATERIALS
LAMINATED CARD

MIKE FAULKNER →DIRECTOR

D-Fuse

D-Fuse
UK – 13-14 GT. SUTTON ST. LONDON. EC1V 0BX. UK.
T +44 (0)20 7253 3462 E info@dfuse.com
JAPAN – AGOSTO, INC.
株式会社アゴスト 〒112 0005東京都文京区水道1-4-6浅野屋ビル3階
BLDG. 1-4-6 SUIDOU, BUNKYO-KU, TOKYO. 112-0005.
T +81 (0)3-5684-4751 F +81 (0)3-5684-2977 E judy@agosto.com

D-Fuse
UK – PO BOX 39943, LONDON. EC1V 0YZ. UK.
T +44 (0)20 7253 3462 E info@dfuse.com
JAPAN – AGOSTO, INC.
株式会社アゴスト 〒112 0005東京都文京区水道1-4-6浅野屋ビル3階
3F ASANOYA BLDG. 1-4-6 SUIDOU, BUNKYO-KU, TOKYO. 112-0005.
T +81 (0)3-5684-4751 F +81 (0)3-5684-2977 E judy@agosto.com

• 07

Heiberger Construction

Woodwork . Design . Custom Carpentry . Project Management . Solar

804.874.4087

HeiArt

Murals . Custom Painting . Faux Finishes

804.874.4087

219
ALR DESIGN
USA
ART DIRECTOR
NOAH SCALIN
DESIGNER
NOAH SCALIN
CLIENT
PETE HEIBERGER

MIKE campbell
mc@thinkcfd.com

www.THINKCFD.COM

liNa

liNa@linaedin.com

197 henry street • san francisco • california • 94114   www.linaed

liN

220
LINA
USA
ART DIRECTOR
LINA EDIN
DESIGNER
LINA EDIN
CLIENT
LINA
PAPER/MATERIALS
COVER STOCK; SATIN FINISH

CF D

602 955 2707

fax. 602 955 2878
cell. 602 390 5799

CAMPBELL FISHER **DESIGN**
3333 E CAMELBACK STE 200 PHX AZ 85018

THE GLOBAL ILLUSTRATION CORPORATION

JONES **BRAY** DAVIES

OFFICE STUDIO SQUAT

6 MIDDLETON PLACE LONDON W1W 7TE

THE GLOBAL ILLUSTRATION CORPORATION

JONES ~~BRAY~~ ~~DAVIES~~

OFFICE **STUDIO** ~~SQUAT~~

6 MIDDLETON PLACE LONDON W1W 7TE

J B D

ELECTRONIC POST **EMAIL** PORN HUB

JONESBRAYDAVIES@YAHOO.CO.UK

TELEPHONE **BLOWER** NHS NUMBER O FACSIMILE **FAX** LOTTO NUMBERS

07810 650 762   **020 75 804 266**

J B D

ELECTRONIC POST ~~EMAIL~~ ~~PORN HUB~~

JONESBRAYDAVIES@YAHOO.CO.UK

TELEPHONE **BLOWER** ~~NHS NUMBER~~ O FACSIMILE **FAX** ~~LOTTO NUMBERS~~

07810 650 762   **020 75 804 266**

221
**CAMPBELL FISHER
DESIGN**
USA
ART DIRECTORS
**MIKE CAMPBELL
GREG FISHER**
DESIGNER
GG LEMERE
CLIENT
CAMPBELL FISHER DESIGN

222
UNREAL
UNITED KINGDOM
ART DIRECTORS
**BRIAN EAGLE
DAVID BRAY**
DESIGNERS
**BRIAN EAGLE
DAVID BRAY**
CLIENT
JONES BRAY DAVIES

223
BECKER DESIGN
USA
ART DIRECTOR
NELL BECKER
DESIGNER
NELL BECKER
CLIENT
HIRSCH, WALLERSTEIN, MATLOF + FISHMAN
PAPER/MATERIALS
NEENAH CLASSIC CREST

HIRSCH   WALLERSTEIN   MATLOF $^+$ FISHMAN LLP

David J. Matlof
Attorney at law

10100 Santa Monica Boulevard, 23rd Floor
Los Angeles, California 90067
phone 310 712-6473 fax 310 712-6199
dmatlof@hwmfesq.com

HWM $^+$ F

224
MIRIELLO GRAFICO, INC.
USA
DESIGNER
SALLIE REYNOLDS
CLIENT
ESSEL ENTERPRISES
PAPER/MATERIALS
DUPLEXED 80# CARNIVAL COVER COCO

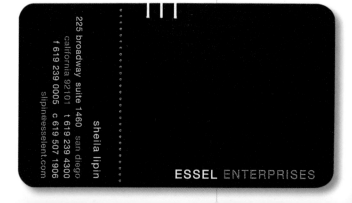

sheila lipin

225 broadway suite 1460 san diego
california 92101   t 619 239 4300
f 619 239 0005 c 619 507 1906
slipin@esselent.com

ESSEL ENTERPRISES

centro

monte athos 145, lomas de chapultepec
cp 11000 méxico df, tel. 5202 6017 | 4779
5520 4159 | 4152 | 8686 fax. 5520 8386
www.centro.org.mx, jbolado@centro.org.mx

JORGE BOLADO

225

BLOK DESIGN
MEXICO

ART DIRECTOR
VANESSA ECKSTEIN

DESIGNERS
VANESSA ECKSTEIN
MARIANA CONTEGNI

CLIENT
CENTRO

PAPER/MATERIALS
FOX RIVER; SIRIUS SMOOTH

PERSONAL NOTE:

Ph. 415.
305.5264

ASHTON CATES
☐ dj ☐ Architect ☐ friend

522 FELL No. 3
SAN FRANCISCO
CALIFORNIA 94102

www.workr.com

226

LINA
USA

ART DIRECTOR
LINA EDIN

DESIGNER
LINA EDIN

CLIENT
ASHTON CATES

PAPER/MATERIALS
FINCH VANILLA; COVER 100#

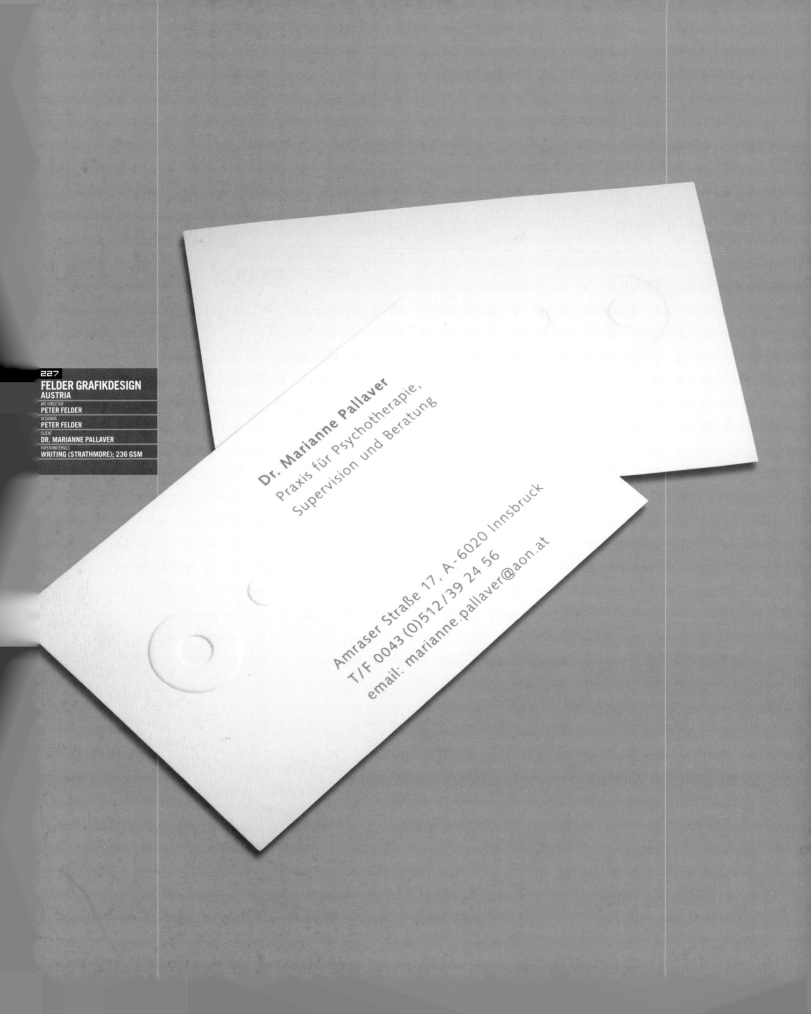

Dr. Marianne Pallaver
Praxis für Psychotherapie,
Supervision und Beratung

Amraser Straße 17, A-6020 Innsbruck
T/F 0043 (0)512/39 24 56
email: marianne.pallaver@aon.at

228
BRUKETA & ZINIC
CROATIA
ART DIRECTOR
SINISA SUDAR
DESIGNER
SINISA SUDAR
CLIENT
BRANDUCTOR
PAPER/MATERIALS
LAKE EXTRA 350

BRANDOCTOR⊕
BRUKETA&ŽINIĆ O.M.

ANJA BAUER *SENIOR BRAND CONSULTANT
ZAVRTNICA 17, 10 000 ZAGREB, CROATIA
T. + 385 1 6192 597, F. + 385 1 6064 001,
T. + 385 1 6192 598, M. + 385 98 429 062
ANJA@BRANDOCTOR.COM, WWW.BRANDOCTOR.COM

229
PURE
USA
ART DIRECTOR
AARON KING
CLIENT
SELF-PROMOTION

DAVID SCHULENBURG PRODUCER
DAVID@PURENY.COM

99 MADISON AVENUE FLOOR 4 NEW YORK, NY 10016 P212.213.2200 F212.213.2309 WWW.PURENY.COM

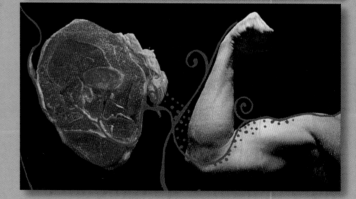

93   04   70   98

 jo lo 盧宇軒 design director   *full member, hkda*

www.**zeroart**studio.com   jolo@zeroartstudio.com
workshop: 1/f, 73 hin tin village, shatin, hong kong
mail: p.o.box 71466 kowloon central post office hong kong
tel. +852 26 09 40 60 fax. +852 26 09 40 50
china mobile 1353 88 44 66 0

230
ZEROART STUDIO
HONG KONG
ART DIRECTOR
JO LO
DESIGNER
NICOLE CHU
CLIENT
ARTIST SALON
PAPER/MATERIALS
**210 GSM ART CARD WITH GLOSS
LAMINATION ON FRONT**

Hochschule für Künste
University of the Arts
Bremen

Dechanatstraße 13 – 15
28195 Bremen

Prof. Thomas Mohr
Gesang
tmohr@t-online.de

www.hfk-bremen.de

231
**HOCHSCHULE FÜR
KÜNSTE BREMEN**
GERMANY
ART DIRECTOR
DANIEL HENRY BASTIAN (TUTOR)
DESIGNER
JULIAN HIELSCHER (STUDENT)
CLIENT
**HOCHSCHULE FÜR KÜNSTE,
UNIVERSITY OF THE ARTS BREMEN**
PAPER/MATERIALS
MUNKEN LYNX 240 GSM

Design Nut 3716 Lawrence Ave. Kensington, MD 20895
t: 301.942.2360 f: 301.942.2361 www.DesignNut.com

Brent M. Almond Principal/Creative Director
e: Brent@DesignNut.com

232
DESIGN NUT, LLC
USA
ART DIRECTOR
BRENT M. ALMOND
DESIGNER
BRENT M. ALMOND
CLIENT
DESIGN NUT, LLC
PAPER/MATERIALS
120# PRODUCTION DULL COVER

DEREK JOHNSON
illustration and product design
CORSO DI PORTA ROMANA 129
20122 MILANO, ITALY, EU
tel: ++ (39) 02 365 55 449
derek.johnson@blueshape.com

233
BLUESHAPE
USA
ART DIRECTOR
DEREK JOHNSON
DESIGNER
DEREK JOHNSON
CLIENT
SELF-PROMOTION
PAPER/MATERIALS
MICRO-INJECTION PLASTIC

%

PAUL
WU
+
ASSOCIATES
chartered accountants

604,734,7750

Paul S.P. Wu
CA

Paul Wu + Associates Ltd.

3320 Quebec Street
Vancouver, BC
V5V 4Z8 Canada

t 604.734.7750
f 604.734.0783
e paulwu@paulwu.ca

234
NANCY WU DESIGN
CANADA
ART DIRECTOR
NANCY WU
DESIGNER
NANCY WU
CLIENT
PAUL WU + ASSOCIATES LTD
PAPER/MATERIALS
**BECKET EXPRESSIONS/LITHO
FOIL STAMPING
HANDCUT EDGES WITH CUSTOM
PINKING SHEARS**

235
DIMAQUINA
BRAZIL
ART DIRECTOR
NAKO
DESIGNER
NAKO
CLIENT
OFICINA P:AR
PAPER/MATERIALS
**OFFSET PAPER (250 GSM)
SILKSCREEN**

■ Marcelo Jardim
■   arquiteto • cel 9923 3742 _ marcelo@oficinapar.com.br

oficinap:ar
PROJETOS DE ARQUITETURA

Rua Ataulfo de Paiva, 1251 s 502 _ Leblon
Rio de Janeiro _ 22440-031 _ RJ
tel/fax 55 21 2239-5688 _ www.oficinapar.com.br

KEVIN

~ little ~

artdirector

m 07798 735 651
e kevinroylittle@hotmail.com

236
UNREAL
UNITED KINGDOM
ART DIRECTOR
BRIAN EAGLE
DESIGNER
BRIAN EAGLE
CLIENT
KEVIN LITTLE

237
BELL SPORTS
USA
ART DIRECTOR
CASEY POTTER
DESIGNER
CASEY POTTER
CLIENT
BELL POWER SPORTS
PAPER/MATERIALS
110# PEGASUS BRILLIANT WHITE

Casey Potter
Art Director

T: 831 420 4070
F: 831 457 4444
cpotter@bellsports.com

BELL
HELMETS

Bell Powersports
380 Encinal Street
Santa Cruz, CA 95060

www.bellhelmets.com

Ma
The   Manta Restaurant
6 C   The Wharf Woolloomooloo
Wo   6 Cowper Wharf Road
T 0   Woolloomooloo 2011
F 0   T 02 9332 3822
ma   F 02 9332 3655
         mantarestaurant.com.au

treatment™
トリートメント

Sam Pattinson サム.パティンソン
Producer プロデューサー

M + 44 (0)7956 676 451   Unit 2A Queens Studios
T + 44 (0)20 7644 6596   121 Salusbury Road
F + 44 (0)20 7328 4447   London NW6 6RG
E sam@treatmentuk.com   United Kingdom

www.treatmentuk.com

238

ZIP DESIGN LTD.
UNITED KINGDOM

ART DIRECTOR
PETER CHADWICK
DESIGNER
DAVID BOWDEN
CLIENT
TREATMENT UK

239
EMERYFROST
AUSTRALIA
ART DIRECTOR
VINCE FROST
DESIGNERS
VINCE FROST
ANTHONY DONOVAN
CLIENT
MANTA RESTAURANT
PAPER/MATERIALS
SPICERS BOXBOARD 600 GSM

i-TVST **AG**

240
KEARNEYROCHOLL
GERMANY
ART DIRECTOR
FRANK ROCHOLL
DESIGNER
MICHAEL SCHMIDT
CLIENT
KEARNEYROCHOLL

```
         * * *

  CHRISTOPHER HUPP
    HUPP2@AOL.COM

   P 317 / 698 3781

 ------------------

THEMARKETINGDEPARTMENT.ORG

   PO BOX 501908

  INDIANAPOLIS IN

       46250

         * * *
```

241
LODGE DESIGN CO.
USA
DESIGNER
ERIC KASS
CLIENT
THE MARKETING DEPARTMENT
PAPER/MATERIALS
130# MANILA TAG

Lorgan's
the Retro Store
100E Pasir Panjang Road
#01-03 Century Warehouse
Singapore 118521
Telephone. 6272 4988
Fax. 6276 7988
Mobile. 9455 0133
Email. lorgan@pacific.net.sg
www.lorgans.com

242

KINETIC SINGAPORE
SINGAPORE

ART DIRECTOR
ROY POH

DESIGNER
ROY POH

CLIENT
LORGAN'S, THE RETRO STORE

PAPER/MATERIALS
300 GSM ART CARD WITH DIE-CUTS

Wallie is een initiatief van DCC, onderdeel van de Distri Group

Wallie bv
De Lierseweg 7-9
2291 PD Wateringen
t   0174 389 000
f   0174 389 001
m   06 484 312 64

Thijs Houba
Commercieel Manager

t.houba@wallie-card.nl
www.wallie-card.nl

244
LIZETTE GECEL
USA
DESIGNER
LIZETTE GECEL
CLIENT
LIZETTE GECEL
PAPER/MATERIALS
CHAMPION CARNIVAL

245
KESSELSKRAMER
THE NETHERLANDS
ART DIRECTORS
ERIK KESSELS
KRISTA ROZEMA
CLIENT
DISTRIGROUP HOLDING, BV

243
UP DESIGN BUREAU
USA
ART DIRECTOR
CHRIS PARKS
DESIGNER
CHRIS PARKS
CLIENT
SCOOTER PLANET – KURT STARKS
PAPER/MATERIALS
COUGAR 100#

Margje de Koning /
Regisseur /
Tel: (31)20 6798103 /
Fax: (31)20 6767574 /
Mobile: (31) 6 24608776 /
Hemonylaan 12 /
1074 BG Amsterdam /

Vrouw in actie #16:
De polsblokkage met
achterwaartse armdraai.

Vrouw in actie #03:
De beendruk met
knieklem na knokkelstoot
op handrug.

Vrouw in actie #38:
De schoudertorsie met
beenworp.

246
KESSELSKRAMER
THE NETHERLANDS
ART DIRECTOR
ERIK KESSELS
CLIENT
MARGIE DE KONING

Premium Quality Aromatics & Botanicals

luxuriabotanica

A MODERN APOTHECARY

info@luxuriabotanica.com

1 614 7480406   www.luxuriabotanica.com

247
REDBEAN
USA
ART DIRECTOR
MELISSA CROWLEY
DESIGNER
MELISSA CROWLEY
CLIENT
**LUXURIA BOTANICA: A MODERN
APOTHECARY**
PAPER/MATERIALS
**100% POST-CONSUMER
RECYCLED PAPER
SOY INKS**

248

MAGENTA DESIGN STUDIO
CROATIA

ART DIRECTORS
SANJA PAVLICA
VANJA BLUMENSAJN

DESIGNER
SANJA PAVLICA

CLIENT
IVANA BILANDIJA HENCE BILLY, STYLIST

PAPER/MATERIALS
MUNKEN PRINT 15; 300 GSM

it's really important that you stamp this sober.

oops, you've missed it!

BILLY | inventor of **PINK colour**

not imPRESSED yet? demand your stamp!

+ 385 91 518 333 2

PLUSTRIOSAMPETDEVETJEDAN
PETJEDANOSAMTRITRITRIDVA

➤➤ ivana.bilandzija@zg.htnet.hr

is this card STYLISH or what?

it's really important that you stamp this sober.

if stamped outside the marked area, the card is considered invalid • don't accept previously stamped card. demand a fresh one • abuse this card! bad style can be avoided • this card is a privillege. feel free to brag around with it • if stopped by fashion police use this card as a wild card • use of this card in any obscene or drug related matter is strictly forbbiden • it is NOT a sex toy • if found dead, the owner of this card gives away all his/hers fashion possesions to the person who issued this card • this card is untransferrable. if you've found this card accidently, please return it to the first cool person you see • being stylish isn't easy, but if you like this card, you are half way there

restaurant niçois

de pizza à

1121, Anderson ⚘ Montreal (Qc) H2Z 1M1
t 514.861.7076 f 514.861.8294
chef@nizza.ca ⚘ www.nizza.ca

nizza

249

DULUDE
CANADA

ART DIRECTOR
DENIS DULUDE

DESIGNER
DENIS DULUDE

CLIENT
DE PIZZA À NIZZA

PAPER/MATERIALS
HORIZON

Benjamin Kaubisch

6 ONE 8

2200 ADELINE STREET
NUMBER 335
OAKLAND, CA 94607
P. 415.902.5549
ben@6one8.com
www.6one8.com

800 X 600

1024 X 768

1280 X 800

1600 X 1024

// form that functions //-->

250

RED CANOE
USA

ART DIRECTOR
DEB KOCH

DESIGNER
CAROLINE KAVANAGH

CLIENT
6ONE8

PAPER/MATERIALS
**FRENCH; CONSTRUCTION
PUREWHITE; 70# TEXT**

251
THNK MARKETING
SERBIA & MONTENEGRO
ART DIRECTOR
PREDRAG MATOVIĆ
DESIGNER
PREDRAG MATOVIĆ
PAPER/MATERIALS
250 GSM PAPER

PREDRAG MATOVIĆ / industrijski dizajner

Stevana Đurđevića Trošarinca 1/30

252
ZEIGLER/DACUS
USA
ART DIRECTOR
BEN DACUS
DESIGNER
BEN DACUS
CLIENT
SMALL TOWN MUSIC
PAPER/MATERIALS
100# COVER; SMART CARNIVAL; VELLUM

253
3RD EDGE COMMUNICATIONS
USA
ART DIRECTOR
FRANKIE GONZALEZ
DESIGNER
MICHELLE WANG
CLIENT
THE CITYLINE CHURCH

josué rodriguez
senior pastor

josué@citylinechurch.com
phone 201.332.0970 fax 201.332.0970
1510 john f. kennedy boulevard
jersey city, new jersey 07305
www.citylinechurch.com

114 rue ambroise croizat 93200 st denis france
T +33 (0) 1 55 84 02 50   F +33 (0) 1 55 84 02 63

w espace114.com

paul j somers
president
M +33 (0) 6 07 46 86 03
psomers@espace114.com

ESPACE 114

254
CONCRETE, CHICAGO
USA
ART DIRECTOR
JILLY SIMONS
DESIGNERS
JILLY SIMONS
REGAN TODD
CLIENT
MSP PARIS SAS (ESPACE 114)
PAPER/MATERIALS
NEENAH CLASSIC CREST
SOLAR WHITE 100# COVER

114 rue ambroise croizat 93200 st denis france
T +33 (0) 1 55 84 02 50   F +33 (0) 1 55 84 02 63

w espace114.com

paul j somers
president
M +33 (0) 6 07 46 86 03
psomers@espace114.com

ESPACE 114

JK
VERANSTALTUNGEN
PERSONAL ENERGY COACHING
SEMINARE

JOCHEN KÖHLER
Dipl.-Sportwissenschaftler

Nietzschestraße 42 // 65191 Wiesbaden
Telefon (06 11) 5 28 09 98 // Fax (06 11) 5 28 09 97 // Mobil (01 73) 6 14 04 41
E-Mail: info@jochen-koehler.com // Internet: www.jochen-koehler.com

255
Q
GERMANY
ART DIRECTOR
THILO VON DEBSCHITZ
DESIGNER
MARCEL KUMMERER
CLIENT
JK – JOCHEN KÖHLER

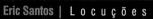

Tel | Fax: 11 3673 5990
Cel: 11 9195 4746
R: Caetés, 878 cj 104
São Paulo, SP
05016-081
ericlsantos@uol.com.br

256
GRAFIKZ
BRAZIL
ART DIRECTOR
ANDREI POLESSI
CLIENT
ERIC SANTOS
PAPER/MATERIALS
COUCHÉ MATTE

SMALLBUTGLOB

Charlie Fisher, Creative
(+45) 41 12 01 64, charl

BUTGLOBAL

257
MUGGIE RAMADANI
DESIGN STUDIO
DENMARK
ART DIRECTOR
MUGGIE RAMADANI
DESIGNER
MUGGIE RAMADANI
CLIENT
SMALLBUTGLOBAL

ipdrum

Kjetil B. Mathisen
Director of Business Development

E-mail: kjetil@ipdrum.com
Mobile: +47 900 25 408
Skype: Baetis

IPdrum as
Bogstadveien 30
N-0355 Oslo, Norway
Phone: +47 23 36 60 80
Fax: +47 22 20 04 10

258

BLUEROOM DESIGN STUDIO
NORWAY

DESIGNERS
LINE R. HAGEN
MARGARETHA ANDREASSEN

CLIENT
IP DRUM

PAPER/MATERIALS
250 GSM SILK

259

HAND MADE SRL
ITALY

ART DIRECTOR
ALESSANDRO ESTERI

DESIGNER
ALESSANDRO ESTERI

CLIENT
LUCIANA ZUFFI (FASHION HOUSE)

PAPER/MATERIALS
ARJO WIGGINS

paolo guidi

italia)

126

IZ

lucianazuffi

LARRY HAMBY >> LARRY@SOUNDFUTURE.COM

SOUNDFUTURE

216 NORTH LUCERNE BOULEVARD   TEL (323) 462.1676
LOS ANGELES, CALIFORNIA 90004   FAX (323) 462.1677
CELL (310) 600.0440   FAX (310) 552.2105

www.soundfuture.com

www.soundfuture.com

261
GIG DESIGN
USA
ART DIRECTOR
LARIMIE GARCIA
DESIGNER
LARIMIE GARCIA
CLIENT
SOUND FUTURE
PAPER/MATERIALS
3/ SPECIAL FLUORESCENT INK

260
BLUEROOM DESIGN STUDIO
NORWAY
DESIGNERS
MARGARETHA ANDREASSEN
LINE R. HAGEN
CLIENT
BLUEROOM
PAPER/MATERIALS
250 GSM SILK

LINE R. HAGEN. GRAPHIC DESIGNER
BLUEROOM DESIGNSTUDIO. OSLO. NORWAY

+

BLUEROOM DESIGNSTUDIO
LINE RENÉE HAGEN. GRAFISK DESIGNER
TEL. +47 930 27 092 / TEL. + 47 909 60 831
WWW.BLUEROOM.NO EMAIL: LINE@BLUEROOM.NO

+

262
HARRIMANSTEEL
UNITED KINGDOM

ART DIRECTOR
HARRIMANSTEEL
DESIGNER
HARRIMANSTEEL
CLIENT
HARRIMANSTEEL
PAPER/MATERIALS
MELLOTEX BRILLIANT WHITE

sparks

henrik th. strøm
system developer/ system architect

mob/ 917 55 155
email/ henrik@sparks.no
www.sparks.no

263
BLUEROOM DESIGN STUDIO
NORWAY
DESIGNERS
MARGARETHA ANDREASSEN
LINE R. HAGEN
CLIENT
SPARKS
PAPER/MATERIALS
250 GSM SILK

Flash ActionScript/ JavaScript/ XML/ HTML/CSS
Macromedia Flash MX/ Fireworks MX/ Dreamweaver MX

C/C++/ C#/ ASP.NET/ ASP/ Perl/ PHP/ HTML/CSS/ Delphi/
Python/ Bash/ Visual Studio.NET/ Emacs/ MSSQL/ MySQL/
Sybase/ mod_perl/ mod_php

C#/ ASP.NET/ XML/ Lingo/ HTML/ SQL/ Visual Studio.
NET/ MSSQL/ Macromedia Director/ 3D Studio Max

Tonic Design Limited
Fourth Floor
143 Shoreditch High St
London E1 6JE
United Kingdom

+44 (0)20 7033 2888 T
+44 (0)20 7033 0666 F
www.tonic.co.uk

tonic

tonic

...strom your Account Director. If you
...ar a slightly bizarre Swedish accent
...then why not give me a
...f that sounds too
...e an email, you can get
... Hopp!

tonic

Hello, I'm Ad...
I'm usually a...
but if that d...
+44 (0)777...
adrianc@to...
funerals an...

Hello, I used to belong to a Designer called Daniel
Hutchinson. He has now given me to you. This is
probably so you can ring him on +44 (0)20 7033
0670 or on +44 (0)7867 510 569. Then again, you
could write to him at daniel@tonic.co.uk

264
TONIC DESIGN LTD.
UNITED KINGDOM
ART DIRECTOR
RANZIE ANTHONY
DESIGNER
SIM WISHIADE
CLIENT
TONIC DESIGN
PAPER/MATERIALS
SPLENDORGEL 340 GSM

Elmegade 23 tv
DK-2200

København N
Danmark

+45 / 242 10 959

info@rebelhairdesign.dk
www.rebelhairdesign.dk

265

**MUGGIE RAMADANI
DESIGN STUDIO**
DENMARK

ART DIRECTOR
MUGGIE RAMADANI
DESIGNER
MUGGIE RAMADANI
CLIENT
REBEL HAIRDESIGN

stephen **o**. hessler

202.393.8100   soh@sottoesq.com

otto

washington, dc

266
**PENSARÉ DESIGN
GROUP LTD.**
USA
ART DIRECTOR
MARY ELLEN VEHLOW
DESIGNER
MARY ELLEN VEHLOW
CLIENT
STEPHEN O. HESSLER, ESQ.
PAPER/MATERIALS
UNCOATED 2-COLOR

ck & Company

Tel: 212/529_1010
Fax: 212/529_9540
info@trollback.com
www.trollback.com

th Avenue
rk, NY

267
TROLLBÄCK + COMPANY
USA
ART DIRECTORS
**JAKOB TROLLBÄCK
JOE WRIGHT**
DESIGNERS
**JAKOB TROLLBÄCK
JOE WRIGHT**
CLIENT
IN-HOUSE

Zócalo Mall

PHONE (602) 387-5112 FAX (602) 387-5001

2375 East Camelback Road, 5th Floor

Phoenix, Arizona 85016

WEBSITE www.zocalomall.com

268

CAMPBELL FISHER DESIGN
USA

ART DIRECTOR
MIKE CAMPBELL

DESIGNERS
STACY CRAWFORD
ANDY MROZINSKI

CLIENT
ZÓCALO MALL

tel: +52 (55) 52.01.08.10	facsimile: +52 (55) 52.01.08.95
juan manuel pinedo	Blvd. M. Avila Camacho 40 P.24 Colonia Lomas de Chapultepec México D.F., CP 11000, México e-mail: jmpinedo@satmex.com

269

BLOK DESIGN
MEXICO

ART DIRECTOR
VANESSA ECKSTEIN

DESIGNERS
VANESSA ECKSTEIN
MARIANA CONTEGNI

CLIENT
ALTERNA TV

PAPER/MATERIALS
SIRIUS SMOOTH; FOX RIVER

GRAFIKZ
BRAZIL
ART DIRECTOR
ANDREI POLESSI
CLIENT
BRASREAL TÊXTIL LTDA.
PAPER/MATERIALS
COUCHÉ MATTE

Priscila Minutti
priscila@lilasbrasil.com.br

Rua José Monteiro Nunes, 445
Itatiba,. SP 13255-160 **Tel** (11) 4524 6335
www.lilasbrasil.com.br

FOO SAY KEONG
ART DIRECTOR
HP65.9651 5363
SAY@FFURIOUS.COM

fFurious
CREATIVECOMMUNICATIONS+RETAILSHOP

32A SAGO STREET
SINGAPORE 059025
TEL/FAX65.62250887
WWW.FFURIOUS.COM

271
FFURIOUS
SINGAPORE
ART DIRECTOR
LITTLE ONG
DESIGNER
LITTLE ONG
CLIENT
FFURIOUS
PAPER/MATERIALS
250 GSM ART CARD
MATTE LAMINATION

TELEPHONE 651.439.2558

RIVER VALLEY RIDERS
THERAPEUTIC RIDING PROGRAM

TELEPHONE 651.439.2558

RIVER VALLEY RIDERS
THERAPEUTIC RIDING PROGRAM

273
CAPSULE
USA
ART DIRECTOR
BRIAN ADDUCCI
CLIENT
RIVER VALLEY RIDERS
PAPER/MATERIALS
**FRENCH CONSTRUCTION
RECYCLED WHITE**

BLOOM*

BLOOM*

OLE-KRISTIAN WOLD
DAGLIG LEDER

+

P.B. 7051 ST. OLAVSPLASS N-0130 OSLO
WWW.BLOOM-NORGE.NO . E-MAIL: OLE@BLOOM-NORGE.NO
MOB: + 47 92 65 51 37

272
**BLUEROOM DESIGN
STUDIO**
NORWAY
DESIGNERS
**MARGARETHA ANDREASSEN
LINE R. HAGEN**
CLIENT
BLOOM
PAPER/MATERIALS
250 GSM SILK

274
BASE ART CO.
USA
ART DIRECTOR
TERRY ROHRBACH
DESIGNER
TERRY ROHRBACH
CLIENT
BASE ART CO.
PAPER/MATERIALS
OPUS 100# DULL COVER

TERRY ROHRBACH

BASE ART CO. 623 HIGH STREET

WORTHINGTON OH 43085

T 614 841 7480   F 614 841 7481

TBACH@BASEARTCO.COM

WWW.BASEARTCO.COM

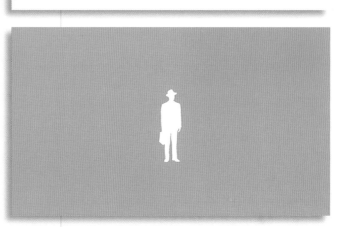

mark

ark

ail@mark-wood.net 07748966810

275
MARK WOOD
UNITED KINGDOM
DESIGNER
MARK WOOD
CLIENT
MARK WOOD
PAPER/MATERIALS
WOOD
HEAT FROM GAS HOB

274
BASE ART CO.

_ photo grA

a
ph y

photo grAphy

Ann e. cutting

one eighty-eight south delAcy Ave
pAsAdena cA 91105
ph_626_440_1974
fx_626_577_8036
ann@cutting.com
www.cutting.com

279
GRAPHICULTURE
USA
DESIGNER
CHAD OLSON
CLIENT
ANN E. CUTTING

278
GRAFIKSTUDIO-STEINERT
GERMANY
DESIGNER
MICHAEL STEINERT
CLIENT
SCHLICHTHERLE & HORST GBR,
CINATRA

Martin Horst
mh@cinatra.de

Hernerstrasse#14   d-44787 Bochum   Mobil: 0049-0172-8520742

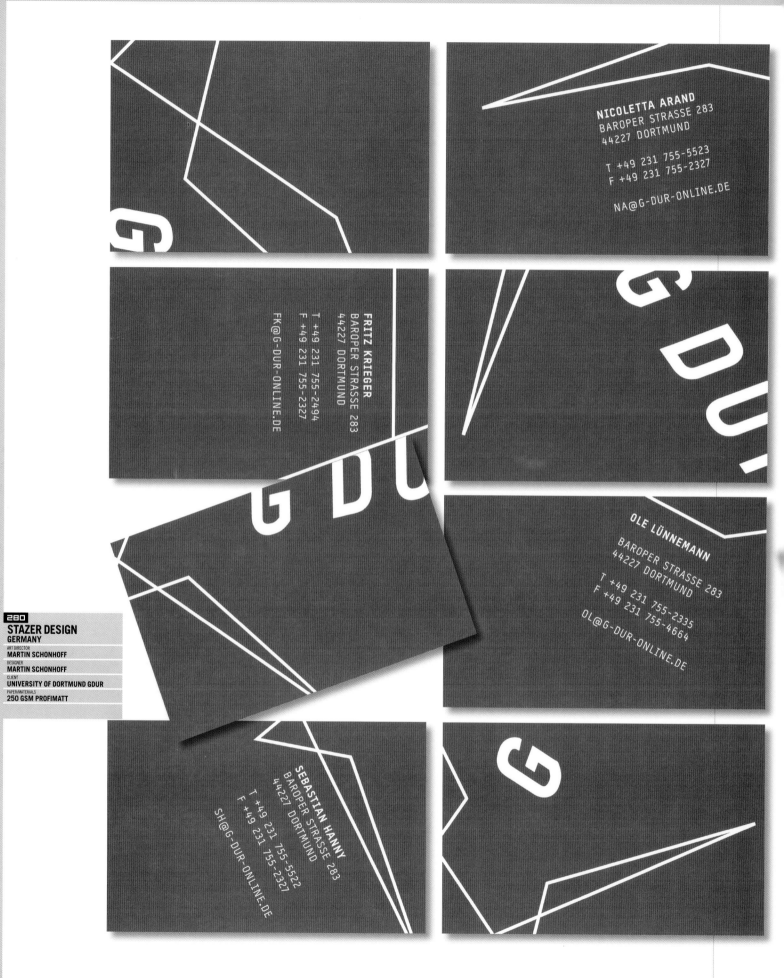

NICOLETTA ARAND
BAROPER STRASSE 283
44227 DORTMUND

T +49 231 755-5523
F +49 231 755-2327

NA@G-DUR-ONLINE.DE

FRITZ KRIEGER
BAROPER STRASSE 283
44227 DORTMUND

T +49 231 755-2494
F +49 231 755-2327

FK@G-DUR-ONLINE.DE

OLE LÜNNEMANN
BAROPER STRASSE 283
44227 DORTMUND

T +49 231 755-2335
F +49 231 755-4664

OL@G-DUR-ONLINE.DE

SEBASTIAN HANNY
BAROPER STRASSE 283
44227 DORTMUND

T +49 231 755-5522
F +49 231 755-2327

SH@G-DUR-ONLINE.DE

280
STAZER DESIGN
GERMANY
ART DIRECTOR
MARTIN SCHONHOFF
DESIGNER
MARTIN SCHONHOFF
CLIENT
UNIVERSITY OF DORTMUND GDUR
PAPER/MATERIALS
250 GSM PROFIMATT

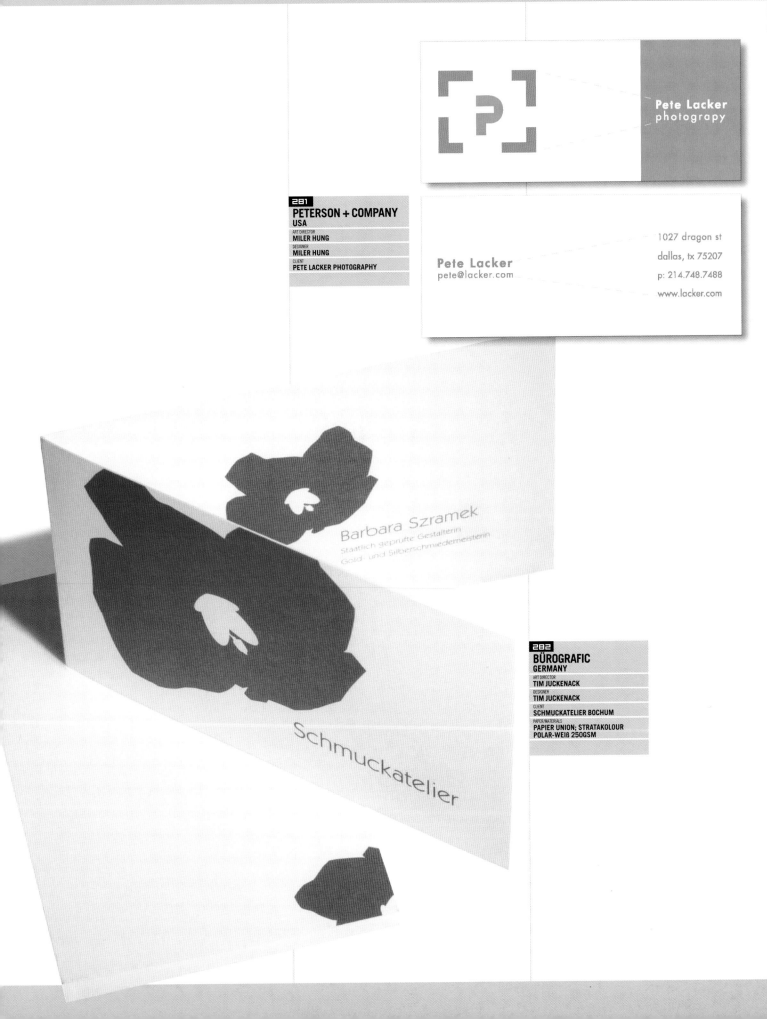

Pete Lacker
photograpy

Pete Lacker
pete@lacker.com

1027 dragon st

dallas, tx 75207

p: 214.748.7488

www.lacker.com

281
PETERSON + COMPANY
USA
ART DIRECTOR
MILER HUNG
DESIGNER
MILER HUNG
CLIENT
PETE LACKER PHOTOGRAPHY

Barbara Szramek
Staatlich geprüfte Gestalterin
Gold- und Silberschmiedemeisterin

Schmuckatelier

282
BÜROGRAFIC
GERMANY
ART DIRECTOR
TIM JUCKENACK
DESIGNER
TIM JUCKENACK
CLIENT
SCHMUCKATELIER BOCHUM
PAPER/MATERIALS
**PAPIER UNION; STRATAKOLOUR
POLAR-WEIß 250GSM**

Nassar Design / 11 Park Street
Suite 1 / Brookline MASS. 02446
T 617 264.2862   F 617 264.2861
n.nassar@verizon.net

Nélida Nassar

283
NASSAR DESIGN
USA
ART DIRECTOR
NÉLIDA NASSAR
DESIGNER
MARGARITA ENCOMIENDA
CLIENT
NASSAR DESIGN
PAPER/MATERIALS
REICH PAPER; CHARTHAM
TRANSLUCENTS; PLATINUM #30

101 Prestwick Estate Way SE
Calgary, AB T2Z 3Y9
403.585.5894
mhannay@shaw.ca

Michele Hannay
ergonomist

284
SAMATAMASON
CANADA
ART DIRECTOR
PAMELA LEE
DESIGNER
PAMELA LEE
CLIENT
MICHELE HANNAY
PAPER/MATERIALS
110# COVER FRASER SYNERGY
SMOOTH PURE WHITE

It's a Learning Curve™

Andrew Long 9 Kirkfields, Baildon
West Yorkshire BD17 6XN
Mobile +44 (0)7775 543871
Telephone +44 (0)1274 590538
Email andrew.long@lineone.net
www.itsalearningcurve.co.uk

286
THOMPSON
UNITED KINGDOM
ART DIRECTOR
IAN THOMPSON
DESIGNER
STEVE WILLS
CLIENT
IT'S A LEARNING CURVE
PAPER/MATERIALS
**CONQUEROR DIAMOND WHITE
WOVE 300 GSM**

285
REACTOR STUDIO
USA
ART DIRECTOR
CLIFTON ALEXANDER
CLIENT
RADIANCE LIGHTWORKS
PAPER/MATERIALS
12 PT. KROMEKOTE

Radiance
Lightworks

Clifton Alexander
principal designer

ph 323.525.1120
fx 323.525.1122
clay@radiancelightworks.com

the art of illumination

www.radiancelightworks.com

1800 N. Highland Ave•5th Floor•Suite 506•Hollywood, CA 90028

Michel Praeger
Scénariste – Dialoguiste
AUTEUR
72 Bd de Bercy, 75012 Paris.
Tél 43 29 97 27 – 43 45 37 12

287
FABRICE PRAEGER
FRANCE
ART DIRECTOR
FABRICE PRAEGER
DESIGNER
FABRICE PRAEGER
CLIENT
MICHEL PRAEGER
PAPER/MATERIALS
COATED

288
EGGERS + DIAPER
GERMANY
ART DIRECTOR
BIRGIT EGGERS
DESIGNER
BIRGIT EGGERS
CLIENT
MERENS INTERIEUR-ARCHITEKT

ı:ı E R E N S
interieurarchitect

marina merens · utrechtsedwarsstr. 30b · 1017 WG Amsterdam
tel 020 427 9883 · fax 020 427 3305 · merens@compuserve.com

ı:ı E R E N S
interieurarchitect

marina merens · utrechtsedwarsstr. 30b · 1017 WG Amsterd
tel 020 427 9883 · fax 020 427 3305 · merens@compuserve.c

kevin jackson, production manager
kevinj@la.primarycolor.com

PR1MARY

5750 Hannum Avenue **CULVER CITY** CA 90230
T 310 841 0250 F 310 841 0254

www.primarycolor.com

289
PH.D
USA
ART DIRECTORS
MICHAEL HODGSON
CLIVE PIERCY
DESIGNERS
MICHAEL HODGSON
CLIVE PIERCY
CLIENT
PRIMARY COLOR
PAPER/MATERIALS
MOHAWK OPTIONS; TRUE WHITE;
100# DTC

clearw˙re

HIGH-SPEED INTERNET MADE SIMPLE. *WAY SIMPLE.*

T: 904 482 1414
F: 904 482 1888
M: 904 631 9643

www.clearwire.com

290
HORNALL ANDERSON
DESIGN WORKS
USA
ART DIRECTORS
JOHN ANICKER
JACK ANDERSON
DESIGNERS
JOHN ANICKER,
LEO RAYMUNDO
SONJA MAX
ANDREW WICKLUND
CLIENT
CLEARWIRE
PAPER/MATERIALS
DOMTAR SOLUTIONS CARRARA WHITE
SUPERSMOOTH; 100# COVER

JOHN RUBLE, FAIA
partner
jruble@mryarchitects.com

BUZZ YUDELL, FAIA
partner
byudell@mryarchitects.com

933 PICO BLVD
SANTA MONICA, CA
90405
TEL 310 450 1400
FAX 310 450 1403
oorerubleyudell.com

moore ruble yudell

933 PICO BLVD
SANTA MONICA, CA
90405
TEL 310 450 1400
architects & planners   FAX 310 450 1403
www.moorerubleyudell.com

291
AUFULDISH & WARINNER
USA
DESIGNER
BOB AUFULDISH
CLIENT
AUFULDISH & WARINNER
PAPER/MATERIALS
**CRANES 110# FLUORESCENT
WHITE WOVE**

TIMOTHY

#2244 EAST V
PHOEN

oxygen design +
communications

401 Richmond St W
Suite 430, Toronto
Ontario M5V 3A8

tel 416 506 0_20_2 x23
fax 416 506 170$_2$
jennifer@oxygen.ca
oxygen.ca

oxygen

Jennifer Weaymouth RGD
SENIOR DESIGNER + ASSOCIATE

292
**OXYGEN DESIGN +
COMMUNICATIONS**
CANADA
ART DIRECTOR
ALEX WIGINGTON
DESIGNER
ALEX WIGINGTON
CLIENT
OXYGEN DESIGN + COMMUNICATIONS
PAPER/MATERIALS
MOHAWK SUPERFINE

living and breathing design™

RYTON

P 602.432.3023   F 602.923.3343

AVENUE
ZONA 85028

TOO@WINDWARD-OM.COM

WINDWARD-OM

294
**CAMPBELL FISHER
DESIGN**
USA
ART DIRECTOR
MIKE CAMPBELL
DESIGNER
WARD ANDREWS
CLIENT
WINDWARD-OM

293
SILVER LINING DESIGN
USA
ART DIRECTOR
TRISH LEAVITT
DESIGNER
TRISH LEAVITT
CLIENT
VANESSA MORRIS
PAPER/MATERIALS
14 PT. GLOSS STOCK

617 953 9184

piano / voice
* VANESSA MORRIS

295
NASSAR DESIGN
USA
ART DIRECTOR
NÉLIDA NASSAR
DESIGNER
MARGARITA ENCOMIENDA
CLIENT
RMA PHOTOGRAPHY
PAPER/MATERIALS
STRATHMORE HEAVY SMOOTH 120#

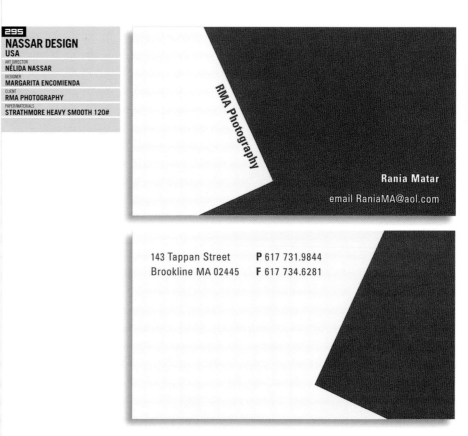

RMA Photography

Rania Matar

email RaniaMA@aol.com

143 Tappan Street   **P** 617 731.9844
Brookline MA 02445   **F** 617 734.6281

THE CUDDLY TOYS
Pee&Poo™

EMMA MEGITT
CEO / Designer
Kiss&Bajs i Sverige AB
Bellmansgatan 8, SE-118 20 Stockholm
Tel: +46 8 642 49 00, Mob: +46 709 53 67 65
emma@peeandpoo.com | www.peeandpoo.com

296
KISS&BAJS AB
SWEDEN
ART DIRECTOR
EMMA MEGITT
DESIGNER
EMMA MEGITT
CLIENT
PEE&POO

297
FREE ASSOCIATION
USA
ART DIRECTOR
JASON FAIRCHILD
DESIGNER
JASON FAIRCHILD
CLIENT
FREE ASSOCIATION
PAPER/MATERIALS
**ASTROLITE PC 100
HAND-PRESSED RECYCLED
NEWSPAPER**

298

OCTAVO
AUSTRALIA

ART DIRECTOR
GARY DOMONEY

CLIENT
25SEVEN ARCHITECTS

PAPER/MATERIALS
360 GSM WHITE A ARTBOARD
MATTE FILM LAMINATION
FOIL STAMP

+ 3 Francis Street South Melbourne Victoria 3205 Australia
T +61 3 9690 0080 **F** +61 3 9690 0280 **M** 0409 694 239
E sdm@25seven.com.au **W** www.25seven.com.au

Steven Mitchell Architect
B.Arch, B.Des.St, RAIA

R O U T L
M O D I S
M O S S
M O R R I S

299

ENTERPRISE IG
SOUTH AFRICA

ART DIRECTOR
DAVE HOLLAND

DESIGNERS
DAVE HOLLAND
ADAM BOTHA

CLIENT
ROUTLEDGE MODISE MOSS MORRIS,
ATTORNEYS

PAPER/MATERIALS
NATURALIS ARCTIC WHITE 330 GSM

FATHIMA KAHN   Associate

Tel 011 286 6900 Fax 011 286 6901 Direct 011 286 6919
Cell 084 437 8601 email FathimaK@routledges.co.za

2 Pybus Road (Cnr Rivonia Road) Sandton Johannesburg
PO Box 78333 Sandton City 2146
www.routledges.co.za

300
GRAPHISCHE FORMGEBUNG
GERMANY
ART DIRECTOR
HERBERT ROHSIEPE
DESIGNER
HERBERT ROHSIEPE
CLIENT
DR. HANS PETER STEINGASS, PSYCHOLOGIST
PAPER/MATERIALS
ARJO WIGGINS IMPRESSIONS RIVES ARTIST SENSATIONS

DIPLOMPSYCHOLOGE

Dr. Hans-Peter Steingass

Katernberger Schulweg 136
42113 Wuppertal

T 02 02.7 67 01 99
M 01 77.6 23 39 61
F 02 02.7 67 01 09
E hp.steingass@t-online.de

301
YANEK IONTEF
ISRAEL
ART DIRECTOR
YANEK IONTEF
DESIGNER
YANEK IONTEF
CLIENT
YANEK IONTEF
PAPER/MATERIALS
MACROMEDIA FREEHAND

+972 (3) 537
+972 (3) 687

iontef
visual communication

yanek iontef
6 keshet street #33
qiryat ono 55401
israel

yanek@netvision.net.il

יונטף
תקשורת חזותית

yanek@netvision.net.il

יאנק יונטף
רחוב קשת 6 / 33
קרית אונו
55401 מיקוד

03 537 1476
+03 687 1681

302

SUBSTANCE151
USA

ART DIRECTORS
IDA CHEINMAN
RICK SALZMAN

DESIGNERS
IDA CHEINMAN
RICK SALZMAN

CLIENT
SUBSTANCE151

PAPER/MATERIALS
FRASER GENESIS CYPRESS VELLUM 2/0
2 HITS OF METALLIC SILVER 877

303

BÜROGRAFIC
GERMANY

ART DIRECTOR
TIM JUCKENACK

DESIGNER
TIM JUCKENACK

CLIENT
BÜROGRAFIC

PAPER/MATERIALS
PAPIER UNION; KEAYKOLOUR
PARZELLAN 300G

151
substance

IDA CHEINMAN CREATIVE DIRECTOR
2304 East Baltimore Street Baltimore, Maryland 21224
410 732 8379 f. 1 425 940 7800 ida.cheinman@verizon.net
www.substance151.com

tim juckenack / bürografic
hattinger straße 764 / 44879 bochum
fon 02 34 - 3 38 62 80 / isdn 02 34 - 3 38 62 86
mail tim@buerografic.com

www.buerografic.de

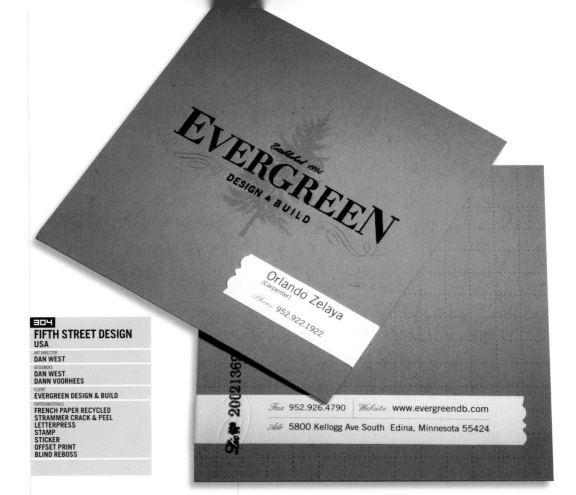

FIFTH STREET DESIGN
USA

ART DIRECTOR
DAN WEST

DESIGNERS
DAN WEST
DANN VOORHEES

CLIENT
EVERGREEN DESIGN & BUILD

PAPER/MATERIALS
FRENCH PAPER RECYCLED
STRAMMER CRACK & PEEL
LETTERPRESS
STAMP
STICKER
OFFSET PRINT
BLIND REBOSS

Ton+Bild
Medientechnik GmbH
Alemannenstraße 49
A-6830 Rankweil
T +43 (0) 55 22 / 48 820
F +43 (0) 55 22 / 48 821
e-mail: tonbild@vol.at

Vermietung, Verkauf
und Service von Audio-
und Videotechnik, Messe-,
Event- und Ausstellungs-
ausstattungen

FELDER GRAFIKDESIGN
AUSTRIA

ART DIRECTOR
PETER FELDER

DESIGNER
PETER FELDER

CLIENT
TON+BILD/MARTIN BECK

PAPER/MATERIALS
OFFSET PAPER; 250 GSM

310 301 0004 FAX 310 301 0177

SCANNING IMAGE ASSEMBLY FILM OUTPUT COLOR PROOFING MULTI
COLOR PRINTING EMBOSSING DIE CUTTING FOIL STAMPING EYELETTING
SCORE DRILL PUNCH PERFORATE NUMBER PADDING SADDLE STITCH
TABBING MOUNTING LAMINATION GUMMING PERFECT BIND HINGING
WIRE-O SPIRAL BIND ENVELOPE CONVERTING HAND ASSEMBLY SOY INKS
METALLIC INKS FLORESCENT INKS LASER INKS MATTE & GLOSS VARNISHING

TONY MANZELLA

tonym@foundationpress.com

5418 McCONNELL AVE. LOS ANGELES CA 90066

FOUNDATION
PRESS
PRINTING CO.

306
PH.D
USA

ART DIRECTORS
CLIVE PIERCY
MICHAEL HODGSON

DESIGNERS
CLIVE PIERCY
CAROL KONO-NOBLE
TAMMY DOTSON

CLIENT
FOUNDATION PRESS

PAPER/MATERIALS
QUARKXPRESS

T 662-287-4477 / 800-848-6543   662-287-94

1111 HIGHWAY 72 EAST   POST OFFICE BOX 867   CORINTH

LLBROTHERSINC.CO

BOB RAY
GENERAL MANAGER

TULL BROTHERS INC

307
GOUTHIER DESIGN
USA

ART DIRECTOR
JONATHAN GOUTHIER

DESIGNER
KILEY DEL VALLE

CLIENT
TULL BROTHERS INC.

PAPER/MATERIALS
FRENCH PAPER – SMART WHITE 80# C

tel 504 522 6300 /ax 504 524 6359

winnie hart   email wi

1055 st. charles avenue suite 300

new orleans, la 70130

ISSIPPI 38835

BSPENCER

309
H
USA
ART DIRECTOR
WINNE HART
DESIGNER
WINNE HART
CLIENT
H
PAPER/MATERIALS
ALUMINUM

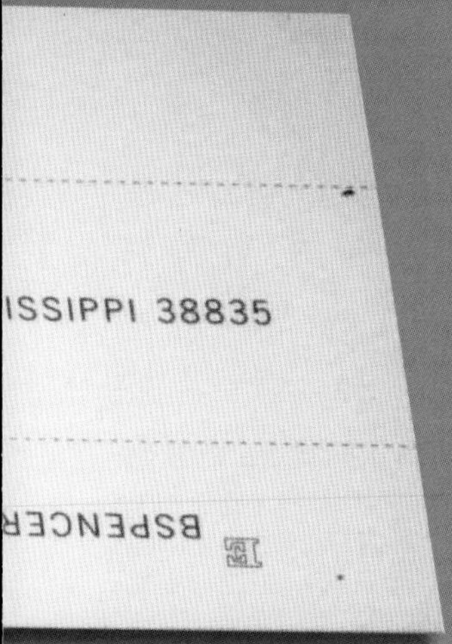

Ben Stott
Creative Director

NB:Studio
24 Store Street
London WC1E 7BA
United Kingdom

T +44 [0]20 7580 9195
F +44 [0]20 7580 9196
b.stott@nbstudio.co.uk

308
NB:STUDIO
UNITED KINGDOM

ART DIRECTORS
ALAN DYE
BEN STOTT
NICK FINNEY
CLIENT
NB:STUDIO

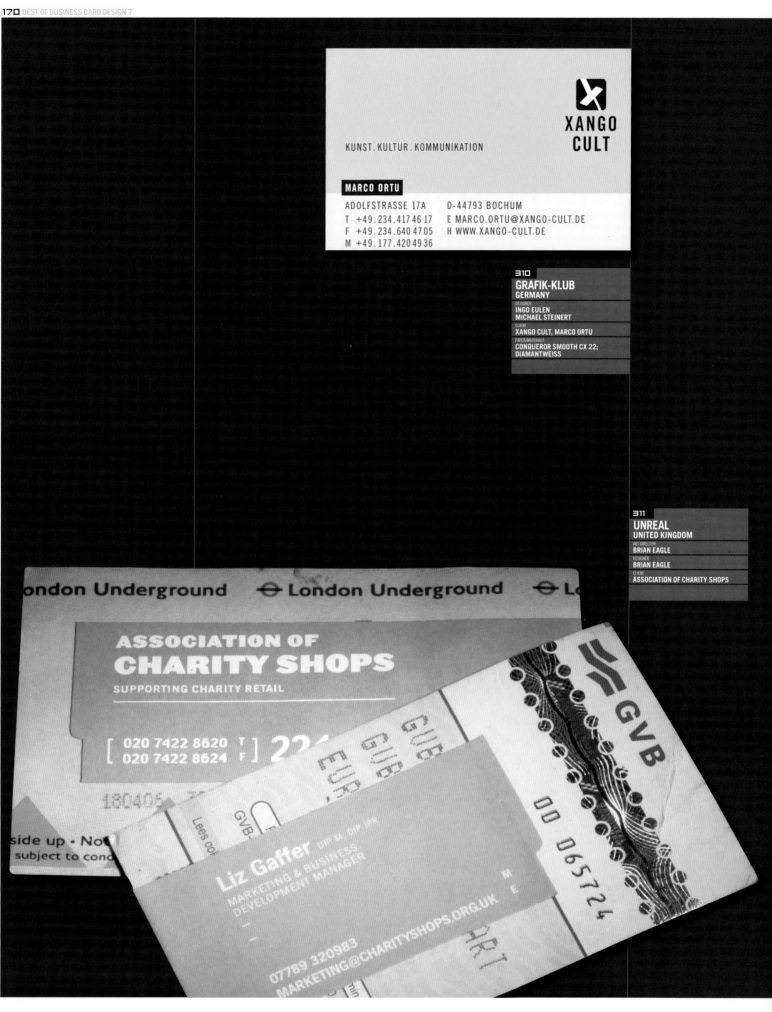

KUNST.KULTUR.KOMMUNIKATION

XANGO CULT

MARCO ORTU

ADOLFSTRASSE 17A   D-44793 BOCHUM
T +49.234.417 46 17   E MARCO.ORTU@XANGO-CULT.DE
F +49.234.640 47 05   H WWW.XANGO-CULT.DE
M +49.177.420 49 36

310

GRAFIK-KLUB
GERMANY
DESIGNER
INGO EULEN
MICHAEL STEINERT
CLIENT
XANGO CULT, MARCO ORTU
PAPER/MATERIALS
CONQUEROR SMOOTH CX 22;
DIAMANTWEISS

311

UNREAL
UNITED KINGDOM
ART DIRECTOR
BRIAN EAGLE
DESIGNER
BRIAN EAGLE
CLIENT
ASSOCIATION OF CHARITY SHOPS

312

HARRIMANSTEEL
UNITED KINGDOM

ART DIRECTOR
HARRIMANSTEEL
DESIGNER
HARRIMANSTEEL
CLIENT
RELATIVE PR
PAPER/MATERIALS
**ROBERT HORNE; MELLOTEX
BRILLIANT WHITE**

RELATIVE PUBLIC RELATIONS IS LOCATED AT
2-30 NOTTINGHAM PLACE LONDON W1M 3FD IF YOU WOULD
LIKE TO TALK TO JUSTINE TELEPHONE +44 171 224 1237
OR FAX HER ON +44 171 224 1237

NESET DESIGN
LOWELL NESET
PRESIDENT/CREATIVE LEAD

323_251_8550
LOWELL@NESETDESIGN.COM
P.O. BOX 480117 LOS ANGELES CA 90048
WWW.NESETDESIGN.COM

313

GEYRHALTER DESIGN
USA

ART DIRECTOR
FABIAN GEYRHALTER
DESIGNER
FABIAN GEYRHALTER
CLIENT
NESET DESIGN
PAPER/MATERIALS
MCCOY

314

EGG CREATIVES
SINGAPORE

ART DIRECTOR
JASON CHEN

DESIGNER
JASON CHEN

CLIENT
URBAN VISUAL

PAPER/MATERIALS
260 GSM BECKETT ENHANCE

urbanvisual
PUTTING SPACE IN PERSPECTIVE

TEO **YOUNG SOON**
DIRECTOR

2A SMITH STREET
SINGAPORE 058917
PHONE 6227 7157   FAX 6227 7537
MOBILE 9685 3043
TYSOON@URBANVISUAL.COM
WWW.URBANVISUAL.COM

DESIGN | 3D VISUALISATION | ANIMATION

urbanvisual

315

RAZOR GROOVE
GRAPHICS
USA

ART DIRECTOR
ROLANDO VILLASEÑOR

DESIGNER
ROLANDO VILLASEÑOR

CLIENT
RAZOR GROOVE GRAPHICS

PAPER/MATERIALS
14 PT. CARD STOCK
4/4 MATTE
SPOT GLASS

ROLANDO VILLASEÑOR
Sr. Graphic Designer

rolando@razorgroove.com
714.206.0985

P.O. Box 654
Westminster,
CA 92683-0654

www.razorgroove.com

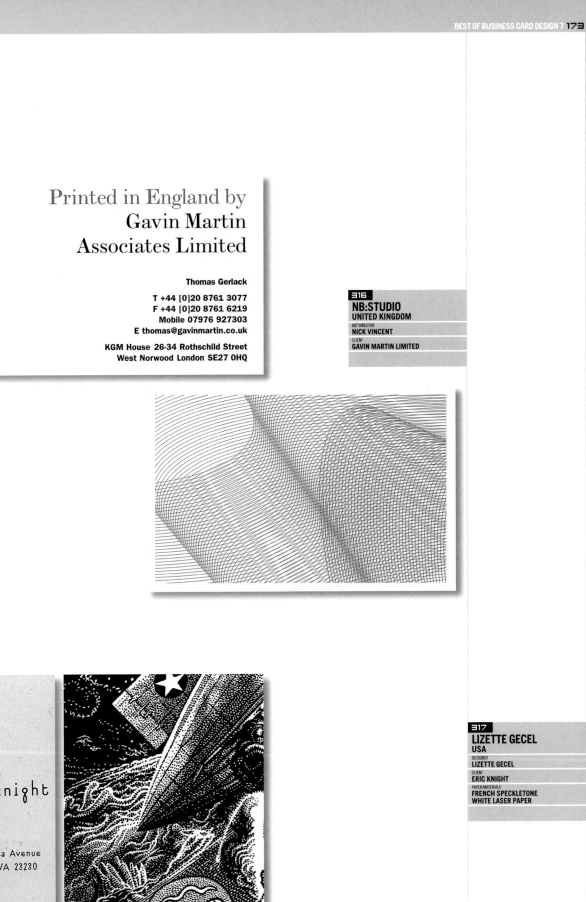

Printed in England by
**Gavin Martin
Associates Limited**

Thomas Gerlack

**T +44 [0]20 8761 3077
F +44 [0]20 8761 6219
Mobile 07976 927303
E thomas@gavinmartin.co.uk**

**KGM House 26-34 Rothschild Street
West Norwood London SE27 0HQ**

**316
NB:STUDIO
UNITED KINGDOM**
ART DIRECTOR
NICK VINCENT
CLIENT
GAVIN MARTIN LIMITED

drawings & collage

eric knight

804 359 1711
4706 Augusta Avenue
Richmond, VA 23230

**317
LIZETTE GECEL
USA**
DESIGNER
LIZETTE GECEL
CLIENT
ERIC KNIGHT
PAPER/MATERIALS
**FRENCH SPECKLETONE
WHITE LASER PAPER**

tricia christiansen
creative director

christiansen : creative

522 2nd Street, Suite 202
Hudson, WI 54016
P 715 381 8480
F 715 381 8498
www.christiansencreative.com
tricia@christiansencreative.com

C

360MODERN.COM LIVING IN MODERN STYLE

Richard Corff managing partner

rcorff@360modern.com
P 425.941.8113   14615 SE 55th St.
F 425.747.1920   Bellevue, Wa 98006

360°modern

360MODERN.COM LIVING IN MODERN STYLE

Joanna Dyckhoff
joanna@360modern.com

360°modern.

P 206.406.2929   PMB 224, 4957 Lakemont Blvd. SE
Bellevue, Washington 98006

Barba

320
CUSP DESIGN
USA
ART DIRECTORS
CHIRANIT PRATEEPASEN
DAVID OLIVER
DESIGNER
CHIRANIT PRATEEPASEN
CLIENT
MERRY MONK DESIGN
PAPER/MATERIALS
MOHAWK SUPERFINE

AMY SANFORD

merry
monk
design

1200 Washington Street, Studio 114
Boston, MA 02118 | Tel 617.698.5174
Email amy@merrymonkdesign.com

Inspiration   considers   the unexpected.

Reason   incorporates   everything.

Imagination   creates   good fortune.

MERRYMONKDESIGN.COM

321
MORTENSEN DESIGN INC
USA
ART DIRECTOR
GORDON MORTENSEN
DESIGNER
SABIHA BASRAJ
CLIENT
BARBARA GIBSON
PAPER/MATERIALS
CANSON WATERCOLOR PAPER

Barbara Gibson [*freelance writing*]   bga@earthlink.net ▪ 251 Loucks Los Altos CA 94022
(P) 650-941-2300 (F) 650-949-3038

692a Moulton ave. LA• CA• 90031

david mocarski

tel: 323 227 0191

fax: 323 227 6172

arkkit@pacbell.net

www.arkkitforms.net

arkkit

forms

david mocarski

furniture
graphics
product
environments

FISCHER-APPELT

19
98

FRITZ
ANTON
CLAUDIA
BERNHARD

¬ St. Benedictstraße 29 ¬ 20149 Hamburg ¬ Telefon 040-410 75 74
¬ e-mail: cfa@ligalux.de ¬ bfa@fischerappelt.de

KARIDIS PRODUCTIONS

HARRY

PHONE (480) 773-6443
FAX (480) 773-7891
EMAIL HARRY@HARRYKARIDIS.COM
26004 NORTH 41st PLACE
PHOENIX, AZ 85050

CTURE
EVERETT, WA 2004

SOVARCHITECTURE
7295 Vashon Hwy. S.W. Suite D2
P.O. Box 1636, Vashon Island, WA 98070
SOVArchitecture.com
463 7701
463 7702

SOVARCHITECTURE
WESTIN GRAND HOTEL: WASHINGTON, D.C. 1996
SOVArchitecture.com

325
**HORNALL ANDERSON
DESIGN WORKS**
USA
ART DIRECTORS
**JACK ANDERSON
LARRY ANDERSON**
DESIGNER
HENRY YIU
CLIENT
SOVARCHITECTURE
PAPER/MATERIALS
MOHAWK SUPERFINE

326
R&MAG GRAPHIC DESIGN
ITALY

ART DIRECTORS
**FONTANELLA
DI SOMMA
CESAR**

CLIENT
R&MAG GRAPHIC DESIGN

327
NB:STUDIO
UNITED KINGDOM

ART DIRECTORS
**ALAN DYE
BEN STOTT
NICK FINNEY**

DESIGNER
CHARLIE SMITH

CLIENT
BLACKWELL + FRIEND

blackwell + friend

richard blackwell
ba(hons) diparch riba

t +44_0_20_7485_5738
f +44_0_20_7485_5741
rb@blackwellfriend.co.uk

blackwell + friend architects
31 oval road
london nw1 7ea
united kingdom

adrian friend
ba(hons) diparch riba

t +44_0_20_7485_5738
f +44_0_20_7485_5741
af@blackwellfriend.co.uk

blackwell + friend architects
31 oval road
london nw1 7ea
united kingdom

Cristine Mortensen
residential garden design

416 bush street mountain view, california 94041
T| 650 965 9531 F| 650 988 0926 cmort@cmdzine.com

APLD certified | association of professional landscape designers

328
MORTENSEN DESIGN INC.
USA
ART DIRECTOR
GORDON MORTENSEN
DESIGNER
ANN JORDAN
CLIENT
CRISTINE MORTENSEN
PAPER/MATERIALS
**CRANE'S FLUORESCENT WHITE
KID FINISH 134# C**

liboristrasse 35

44143 dortmund

germany

fon +49 . 231 . 9598-495

fax +49 . 231 . 9598-494

mobil +49 . 179 . 4 99 64 48

info@stazerdesign.de

MARTIN SCHONHOFF

329
STAZER DESIGN
GERMANY
ART DIRECTOR
MARTIN SCHONHOFF
DESIGNER
MARTIN SCHONHOFF
CLIENT
MARTIN SCHONHOFF
PAPER/MATERIALS
250 GSM MATTE; COATED CELLOPHANE

fin⁺can
HOLZHÄUSER

Ireneus Binczek

Philippstraße 11   T 02234. 936 90 22   M 0163. 88 28 027
50226 Frechen   F 02234. 936 90 23   ireneus@fin-can.de

330
804© GRAPHIC DESIGN
GERMANY
ART DIRECTORS
**HELGE RIEDER
OLIVER HENN**
DESIGNERS
**HELGE RIEDER
OLIVER HENN**
CLIENT
FIN+CAN HOLZHÄUSER
PAPER/MATERIALS
OFFSET AND SCREENPRINTING BILDERDRUCK MATTE

Ambric

IAN GETREU | director of partnership development
| ian@ambric.com

direct 503 601 6505 cell 503 888 2372

Ambric

AMBRIC, INC. | 15655 sw greystone court, suite 150. beaverton, or 97006
main fax
503.601.6500 503.601.6596

GORDON MORTENSEN | PRINCIPAL
650.988.0946 t 650.988.

so**dam**tuff

TUFF MEN + CHICS + ARRANGEMENT + PURPLE

THE BASEMENT 41 PARADISE WALK CHELSEA
LONDON SW3 4JL T +44 020 7351 0111
F +44 020 7352 0001 WWW.SODAMTUFF.COM

334
MORTENSEN DESIGN INC.
USA
ART DIRECTOR
GORDON MORTENSEN
DESIGNER
HELENA SEO
CLIENT
MORTENSEN DESIGN INC.
PAPER/MATERIALS
**CRANE'S FLUORESCENT WHITE
KID FINISH 134# C**

MORTENSEN DESIGN
416 bush st. mountain view, ca 94041   www.mortensendesign.com

(se) arch

Stefanie Eberding Dipl. Ing. (FH), MArch

Architekten   Stephan Eberding und Stefanie Eberding

(AD) Weißenburgstr. 32   (T) 0711 . 640 06 80   (I) team@se-arch.de
        70180 Stuttgart   (F) 0711 . 640 06 81   www.se-arch.de

333
STILRADAR
GERMANY
ART DIRECTORS
**RAPHAEL POHLAND
SIMONE WINTER**
CLIENT
(SE)ARCH, EBERDING ARCHITEKTEN

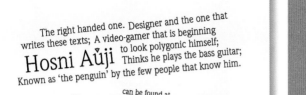

The right handed one. Designer and the one that
writes these texts; A video-gamer that is beginning
Hosni Auji to look polygonic himself;
Thinks he plays the bass guitar;
Known as 'the penguin' by the few people that know him.

can be found at
Telephone +961 3 927380 PenguinCube
PO Box 113-6117, Hamra 1103 2100, Beirut, Lebanon
hosni@penguincube.com

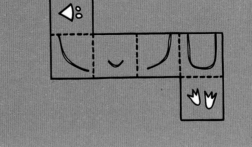

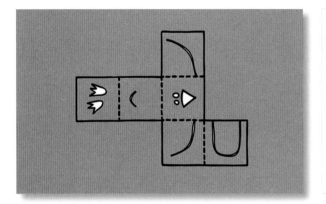

PenguinCube presents
Tammam Yamout
The left handed one. Designer and our PR guy
(probably the one you're talking to); Plays the trombone;
Likes running (a real marathon man); A cube in every sense;
His friends call him 'Timmy' and it seems to have stuck.

Telephone +961 3 937305
PO Box 113-6117, Hamra 1103 2100, Beirut, Lebanon
tammam@penguincube.com

335
PENGUINCUBE
LEBANON
DESIGNER
HOSNI AUJI
TAMMAM YAMOUT
CLIENT
PENGUINCUBE
PAPER/MATERIALS
SPLENDORGEL

336
STOECKER DESIGN
USA
ART DIRECTOR
JAMES STOECKER
DESIGNER
JAMES STOECKER
CLIENT
NANCY BIRSTEIN SMITH
PAPER/MATERIALS
COUGAR 80# MATTE COVER

NANCY HIRSTEIN SMITH
NSNHNHS

|||||||||| NANCY HIRSTEIN SMITH

1023 ROCKROSE AVENUE SUNNYVALE CA 94086

| | | | | | NANCY@HIRSTEIN.COM

408.992.0652 | | | |

337
P2DESIGN
CANADA

ART DIRECTOR
PASCALE PAYANT
DESIGNER
PASCALE PAYANT
CLIENT
DENISE BEAULNE
PAPER/MATERIALS
DOMTAR SOLUTIONS SUPERSMOOTH

denisebeaulne
formationanimation

62, rue Lord Aylmer Gatineau QC J9H 3R7
t : 819.682.3962 c : 819.712.3603
beaulned@sympatico.ca

BUCHANANDESIGN
BOBBY BUCHANAN
5230 CARROLL CANYON ROAD N° 226
SAN DIEGO CA 92121
T 858.450.1150
F 858.450.1160

bobby@buchanandesign.com
www.buchanandesign.com

338
BUCHANAN DESIGN
USA

ART DIRECTOR
BOBBY BUCHANAN
DESIGNER
BOBBY BUCHANAN
CLIENT
BUCHANAN DESIGN
PAPER/MATERIALS
**GILBERT; NEUTECH;
120# BRIGHT WHITE**

339

ZIP DESIGN LTD.
UNITED KINGDOM
ART DIRECTOR
PETER CHADWICK
DESIGNER
DANIEL KOCK
CLIENT
GREEN WOLF FILMS

Rebecca Green
Producer

GREEN WOLF
1-2 Old Barrack Yard
London SW1X 7NP

M 077 6675 3190
T 020 7663 6469
F 020 7663 6364

E rebecca@greenwolf.co.uk
W www.greenwolf.co.uk

www.emda.com

340

JASON AND JASON
ISRAEL
ART DIRECTOR
JONATHAN JASON
DESIGNER
DALIA INBUR
CLIENT
EMDA, HR MANAGEMENT SOLUTIONS
PAPER/MATERIALS
300 GSM CHROME-COATED

EMDA
group
HR Management Solutions

אפי טנדלר
מנכ"ל הקבוצה

לוי אשכול 35, ת.ד 4069
הרצליה פיתוח 46140
טל: 09-9577788
פקס: 09-9570391
efi@emda.com

341
SLANT, INC.
USA
ART DIRECTORS
DAVID SLACK
RYAN GAGNARD
DESIGNER
RYAN GAGNARD
CLIENT
VERAPPRAISE

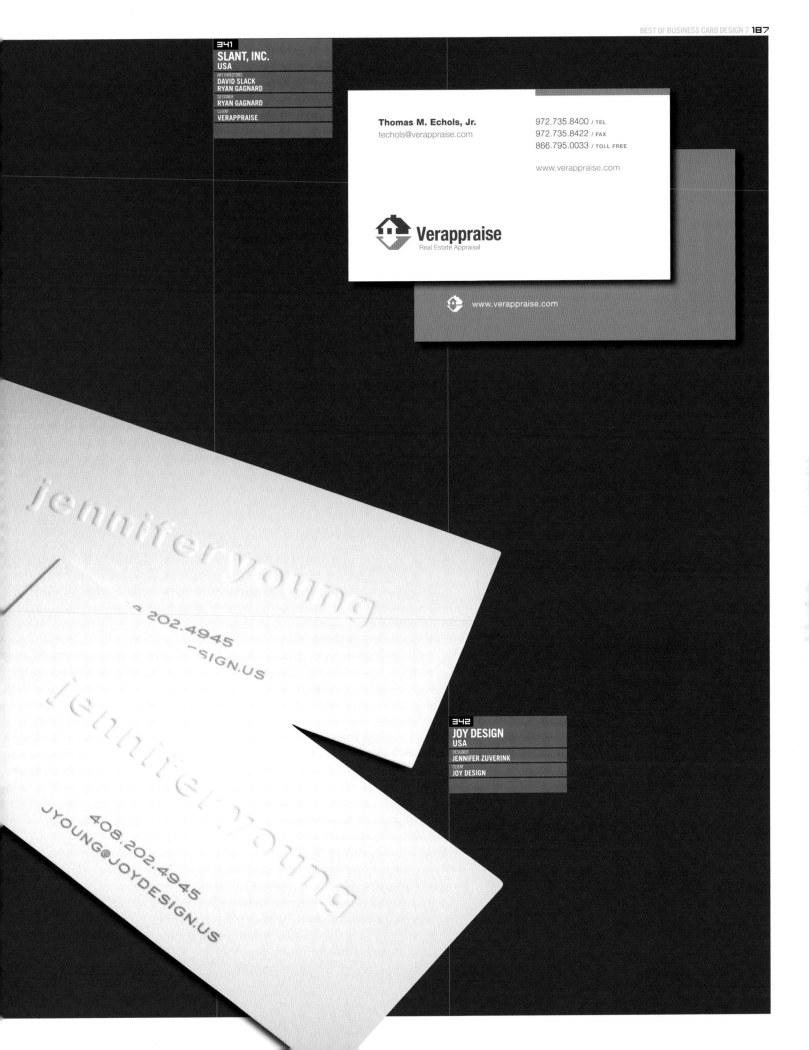

Thomas M. Echols, Jr.
techols@verappraise.com

972.735.8400 / TEL
972.735.8422 / FAX
866.795.0033 / TOLL FREE

www.verappraise.com

Verappraise
Real Estate Appraisal

www.verappraise.com

jenniferyoung

202.4945
SIGN.US

jenniferyoung

408.202.4945
JYOUNG@JOYDESIGN.US

342
JOY DESIGN
USA
DESIGNER
JENNIFER ZUVERINK
CLIENT
JOY DESIGN

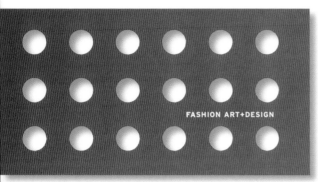

christine barry, ceo

FAD GALLERY

555 SOUTH MAIN STREET PROVIDENCE RI 02903 USA
T. 401 413-5363 F. 401 831-4757
www.fadgallery.com
christine@fadgallery.com

343
PH.D
USA

ART DIRECTORS
CLIVE PIERCY
MICHAEL HODGSON
DESIGNERS
CLIVE PIERCY
CAROL KONO-NOBLE
CLIENT
FAD GALLERY
PAPER/MATERIALS
**MOHAWK NAVAJO; BRIGHT WHITE;
28# WRITING**

verbal by design ®

344
CIRCLE K STUDIO
USA

ART DIRECTOR
JULIE KEENAN
DESIGNER
JULIE KEENAN
CLIENT
DEVIGN, INC. – KAREN NORTH
PAPER/MATERIALS
CLASSIC CREST COVER

Karen North
Principal

devign SM

542 Ralph McGill Blvd NE #6
Atlanta, GA 30312-1120
vox: 404 888 9007
fax: 404 888 9006
karen@devign.com
www.devign.com

Jonathan Lim
Filmmaker/Screenwriter
HP (65) 9630 3188
jonlim@crimsonforestfilms.com

CrimsonForestFilms

345
FFURIOUS
SINGAPORE
ART DIRECTOR
JOANNE TAY
DESIGNER
JOANNE TAY
CLIENT
**CRIMSON FOREST FILMS
(FILM PRODUCTION COMPANY)**
PAPER/MATERIALS
**250 GSM ART CARD
MATTE LAMINATION**

Singapore
...ard Road
...e Paragon
...e 238859
...6735 1511
...5884 4181

Shanghai
Suite 505 Kuen Yang Plaza
798 Zhaojiabang Road
Shanghai 200030
People's Republic of China
Tel (8621) 6473 6112
Fax (8621) 6473 6113

Mexico
Av.Lomas Encanto
#32 B 901
Col. Lomas County Club
Edo. Mexico
Phone (5255) 5290 1404

www.crimsonforestfilms.com

ADAMO LONDON

444
SARATOGA AVENUE, SUITE 2D
SANTA CLARA
CALIFORNIA 95050
FACSIMILE 408 241 7215
www.adamolondon.com

ADAMO LONDON

444
...ATOGA AVENUE, SUITE 2D
...A CLARA
...NIA 95050
...408 241 7215
...amolondon.com

ADAMO LONDO

346
**CHEN DESIGN
ASSOCIATES**
USA
ART DIRECTOR
JOSHUA C. CHEN
DESIGNER
JENNIFER TOLO PIERCE
CLIENT
ADAMO LONDON
PAPER/MATERIALS
CRANE'S 100% COTTON

mark harper
m. 07932 008 225
mark@bonbonlondon.com
www.bonbonlondon.com

348
BONBON LONDON
UNITED KINGDOM
ART DIRECTORS
MARK HARPER
SASHA CASTLING
DESIGNER
MARK HARPER
CLIENT
BONBON LONDON
PAPER/MATERIALS
CURIOUS TOUCH

mais
arquitetura . urbanismo

Fabio Abreu
arquiteto e urbanista

rua barão do rio branco
480 sala 906 centro
governador valadares mg
cep 35010.030
[33]3082.0833
[33]9102.4905

arquiteturamais@yahoo.com.br

347
COMPLEXUS
ARCHITECTURE
AND DESIGN
BRAZIL
ART DIRECTOR
RENATA LA ROCCA
DESIGNER
CLARISSA RIBEIRO
CLIENT
MAIS ARCHITECTURE
PAPER/MATERIALS
COUCHÉ 230 GSM
FILM: DULL
VARNISH: U.V.

Bronwyn Thomas > Public Relations Associate

 MiND INVENTIONS

3950 Third St. N, Suite E   P. 727.898.9900 x 303
St. Petersburg, FL 33703   F. 727.898.9903
                                 bthomas@mindinventions.com

> driving business success through creativity
www.mindinventions.com

driving business success through creativity
www.mindinventions.com

> driving business success through creativity
www.mindinventions.com

349
SUBSTANCE151
USA
ART DIRECTORS
IDA CHEINMAN
RICK SALZMAN
DESIGNERS
IDA CHEINMAN
RICK SALZMAN
CLIENT
MIND INVENTIONS
PAPER/MATERIALS
STRATHMORE ELEMENTS SOLID WHITE;
2-SIDED
3/3 PMS
DIE-CUT

Ph.D

WWW.PHDLA.CO

04 310 .829 .1859

john hughes, Ph.D

15243 cloverfield boulevard,
santa monica, california 904

04 310 .829 .0900 fax 310 .
829 .1859 john@phdla.com

WWW.PHDLA.COM

PRAXISKLINIK FÜR **AUGENHEILKUNDE**

> **DR. ZOLTAN SIMON** | FACHARZT FÜR AUGENHEILKUNDE

ROTEBÜHLPLATZ 19   **T** 0711 . 61 88 55
70178 STUTTGART   **F** 0711 . 61 06 19

ZS@PRAXISKLINIK-FÜR-AUGENHEILKUNDE.DE

| LASERBEHANDLUNGEN

| LASERCHIRURGIE VON FEHLSICHTIGKEITEN

| ALLGEMEINE AUGENHEILKUNDE

350
STILRADAR
GERMANY
ART DIRECTORS
RAPHAEL POHLAND
SIMONE WINTER
CLIENT
PRAXISKLINIK FÜR AUGENHEILKUNDE
(DR. SIMON / DR. SCHNEIDER)

351
PH.D
USA
ART DIRECTORS
CLIVE PIERCY
MICHAEL HODGSON
DESIGNER
CLIVE PIERCY
CLIENT
PH.D
PAPER/MATERIALS
NEW LEAF; EVEREST; 100# COVER

BASE ART CO.
USA

ART DIRECTOR
TERRY ROHRBACH

DESIGNER
TERRY ROHRBACH

CLIENT
BASE ART CO.

PAPER/MATERIALS
OPUS 100# DULL COVER

www.baseartco.com

base art co.

623 high street
worthington, ohio 43085
614 841 7480 tel
614 841 7481 fax
614 327 7375 cell

terry rohrbach
tbach@baseartco.com

Christopher Cannon　　　info@isotope221.com

232 Washington Avenue　　　718.783.3092 *tel*
Fourth Floor　　　　　　　 270.477.6850 *fax*
Brooklyn, NY 11205　　　　 www.isotope221.com

ISOTOPE 221

352

ISOTOPE 221
USA

ART DIRECTOR
CHRISTOPHER CANNON

DESIGNER
CHRISTOPHER CANNON

CLIENT
ISOTOPE 221

PAPER/MATERIALS
**88# COVER STRATHMORE ULTIMATE
WHITE UNCOATED; WOVE FINISH**

<< WWW.EVOLVETECHNOLOGIES.COM

EVOLVE
TECHNOLOGIES

SCOTT HINSHON, CO
SCOTT@EVOLVETECHNOLOGIES.COM

748 LINDEN CIRCLE S.
MAPLEWOOD, MN 55119

P » 651.731.1684
F » 651.739.1186

354
CAPSULE
USA
ART DIRECTOR
BRIAN ADDUCCI
DESIGNER
BRIAN ADDUCCI
CLIENT
EVOLVE TECHNOLOGIES
PAPER/MATERIALS
COUGAR OPAQUE

BRAND BUILDING MERCHANDISE + CONSULTING

MOSQUITO

MICHAEL H PINK

3505 HENNEPIN AVENUE SOUTH
MINNEAPOLIS MINNESOTA 55408
T 612.374.4013   F 612.374.4016

mpink@mosquito-inc.com

355
CAPSULE
USA
ART DIRECTOR
BRIAN ADDUCCI
CLIENT
MOSQUITO
PAPER/MATERIALS
**STRATHMORE WRITING SYSTEM
SOFT BLUE**

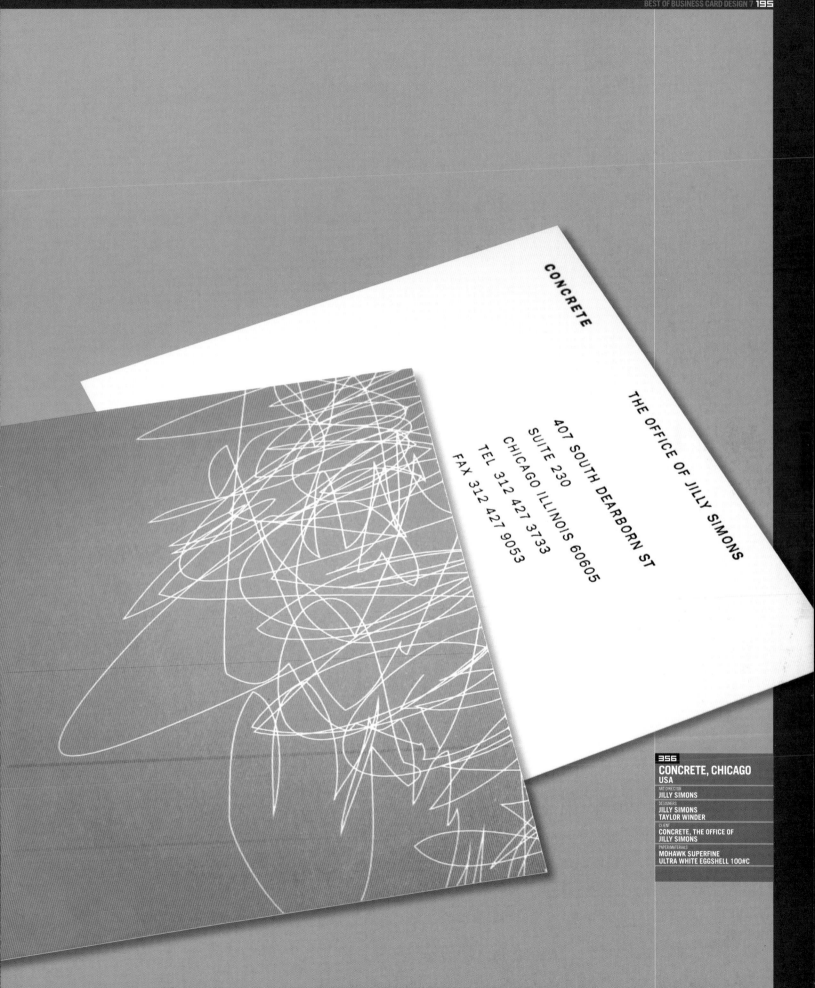

CONCRETE

THE OFFICE OF JILLY SIMONS

407 SOUTH DEARBORN ST
SUITE 230
CHICAGO ILLINOIS 60605
TEL 312 427 3733
FAX 312 427 9053

356

CONCRETE, CHICAGO
USA

ART DIRECTOR
JILLY SIMONS

DESIGNERS
JILLY SIMONS
TAYLOR WINDER

CLIENT
CONCRETE, THE OFFICE OF
JILLY SIMONS

PAPER/MATERIALS
MOHAWK SUPERFINE
ULTRA WHITE EGGSHELL 100#C

357
R&MAG GRAPHIC DESIGN
ITALY
ART DIRECTORS
FONTANELLA
DI SOMMA
CESAR
CLIENT
R&MAG GRAPHIC DESIGN

traversa del pescatore 3
80053 Castellammare di Stabia
info e fax 081 8705053
info@remag.it

Maurizio Di Somma

Marcello Cesar

BEDA

358
GIG DESIGN
USA
ART DIRECTOR
LARIMIE GARCIA
DESIGNER
LARIMIE GARCIA
CLIENT
GIG DESIGN
PAPER/MATERIALS
SATIN LAMINATE STOCK

Gig Design

creative
LARIMIE GARCIA
director

larimie@gigspot.com

209.845.8238
WWW.GIGSPOT.COM
PO BOX 1431 *Oakdale* CALIFORNIA 95361

DAN OGAWA

www.qualityoflife-themovie.com

415 543 5504

FILM PRODUCTION OFFICE
589 Howard Street, Fourth Floor
San Francisco, CA 94105

dan@qualityoflife-themovie.com

359

CHEN DESIGN ASSOCIATES
USA
ART DIRECTOR
JOSHUA C. CHEN
DESIGNER
MAX SPECTOR
CLIENT
QUALITY OF LIFE

360
SATELLITE DESIGN
USA

ART DIRECTOR
AMY GUSTINCIC

DESIGNER
AMY GUSTINCIC

CLIENT
SATELLITE DESIGN

PAPER/MATERIALS
MOHAWK NAVAJO

satellite design •

>	Amy Gustincic
STREET	539 bryant street
SUITE	no. 305
CITY / STATE	san francisco, ca
ZIP CODE	94107
PHONE	415.371.1610
FAX	415.371.0458
EMAIL	amy@satellite-design.com

YOMAR AUGUSTO
:: GRAPHIC ARTIST
www.yvo6.com.br
yo@yvo6.com.br

YOMAR AUGUSTO
:: GRAPHIC ARTIST
www.yvo6.com.br
yo@yvo6.com.br

The business of Metal is to develop
creative projects and help artists and
thinkers put their ideas into action
**Metal can be found at 198a Broadhurst
Gardens West Hampstead London NW6 3AY
Tel: 0207 328 5551 Fax: 0207 328 5552**
Jude Kelly can be reached on 07802 231882
or at jude@metalculture.com

Metal

Sm	Mg	Cc
Stimulation	Meaning	Character
Hm	Rs	Cvt
Humanity	Resolution	Conviction

362

THOMPSON
UNITED KINGDOM

ART DIRECTOR
IAN THOMPSON
DESIGNER
IAN THOMPSON
CLIENT
METAL
PAPER/MATERIALS
**CONQUEROR DIAMOND WHITE
WOVE 300 GSM**

The function of Metal is to create space for
artists and thinkers to develop their ideas and
further the philosophy of their work
**Metal can be found at 198a Broadhurst Gardens
West Hampstead London NW6 3AY
Tel: 0207 328 5551 Fax: 0207 328 5552**
Jude Kelly can be reached on 07802 231882
or at jude@metalculture.com

Metal

Id	Fre	Sm
Ideas	Freedom	Stimulation
Spc	Vsn	Hm
Space	Vision	Humanity

361

VO6
BRAZIL

ART DIRECTOR
YOMAR AUGUSTO
DESIGNER
YOMAR AUGUSTO
CLIENT
VO6
PAPER/MATERIALS
PLASTIC

363
BRUNO PORTO
BRAZIL
DESIGNER
BRUNO PORTO
CLIENT
BRUNO PORTO
PAPER/MATERIALS
**1-COLOR (SILVER) OFFSET PRINT ON
GRANDEE BALBOA BLUE; 216 GSM**

364
KESSELSKRAMER
THE NETHERLANDS
ART DIRECTOR
ERIK KESSELS
CLIENT
ONE 4 TWO

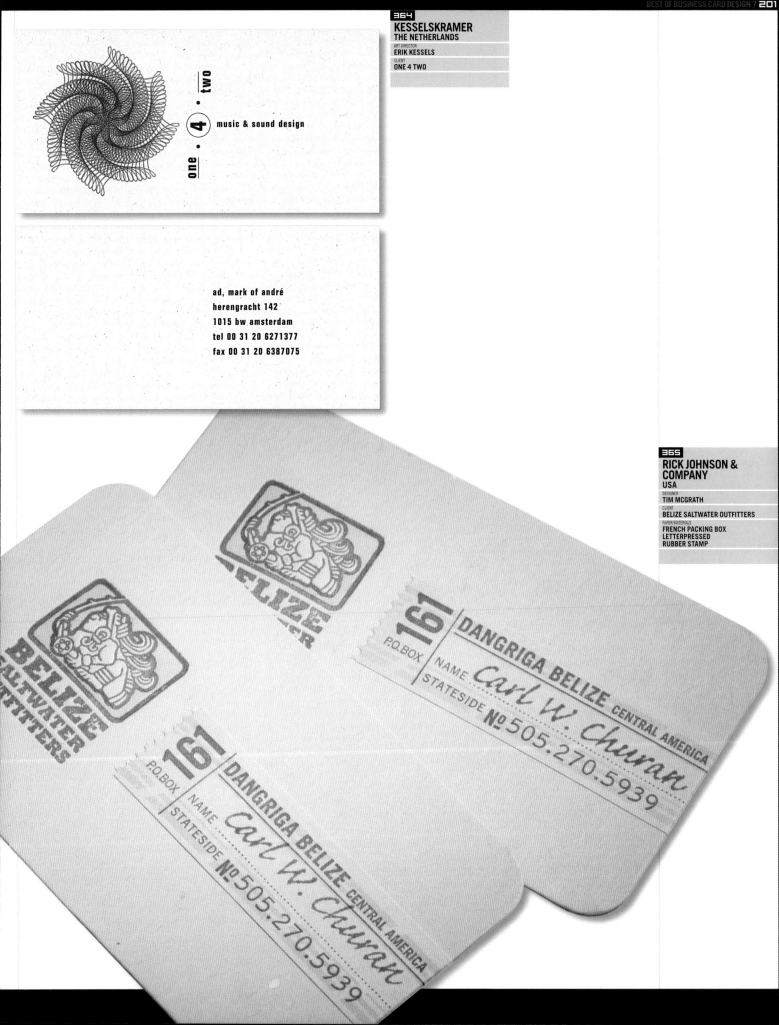

one · **4** · two

music & sound design

ad, mark of andré
herengracht 142
1015 bw amsterdam
tel 00 31 20 6271377
fax 00 31 20 6387075

365
**RICK JOHNSON &
COMPANY**
USA
DESIGNER
TIM MCGRATH
CLIENT
BELIZE SALTWATER OUTFITTERS
PAPER/MATERIALS
**FRENCH PACKING BOX
LETTERPRESSED
RUBBER STAMP**

Peter Felder G
A-6830 Rankv
T 0043(0)552

Peter Felder Grafikdesign
A-6830 Rankweil, Alemannenstraße 49
T 0043(0)5522/45002, F 45020

tahiti

Le Tahiti
bar, restaurant de poissons et de fruits de mer,
situé sur le petit port de Mornac-sur-Seudre,
dans l'un des cent plus beaux villages de France.

1, route de La Seudre. 17113 Mornac-sur-Seudre
Tél : 05 46 22 76 53. Fax : 05 46 02 15 10

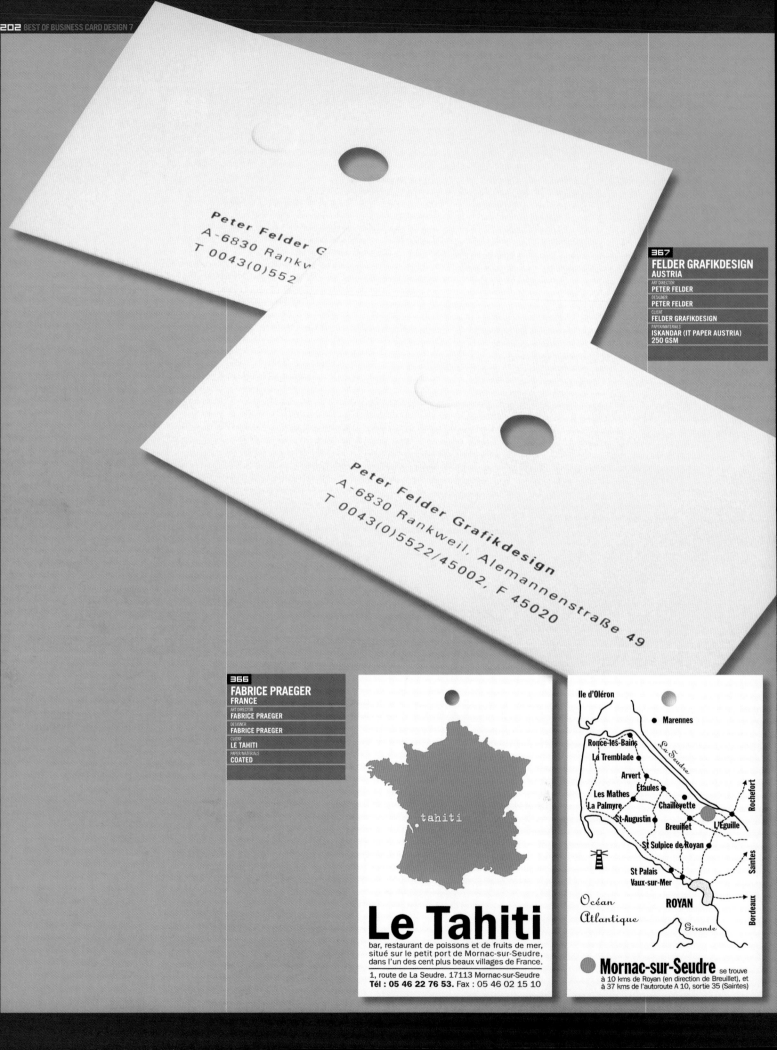

Ile d'Oléron

Marennes

Ronce-les-Bains
La Tremblade

La Seudre

Arvert
Étaules
Les Mathes
La Palmyre
Chailleyette
St-Augustin
Breuillet
L'Eguille

Rochefort

St Sulpice de Royan

Saintes

St Palais
Vaux-sur-Mer

Océan
Atlantique

ROYAN

Bordeaux

Gironde

Mornac-sur-Seudre se trouve
à 10 kms de Royan (en direction de Breuillet), et
à 37 kms de l'autoroute A 10, sortie 35 (Saintes)

carl mazer

415 552 2160
create@carlmazer.com

Hungry?

carl mazer

415 552 2160
create@carlmazer.com

carl mazer

415 552 2160
create@carlmazer.com

carl mazer

415 552 2160
create@carlmazer.com

carl mazer

415 552 2160
create@carlmazer.com

QUALITY MEATS

carl mazer

415 552 2160
create@carlmazer.com

368
CIRCLE K STUDIO
USA
ART DIRECTOR
JULIE KEENAN
DESIGNER
JULIE KEENAN
CLIENT
CARL MAZER
PAPER/MATERIALS
SOMERSET

369

SLANT, INC.
USA

ART DIRECTORS
RYAN GAGNARD
DAVID SLACK
DESIGNER
DAVID SLACK
CLIENT
RD2, INC.

370

SLANT, INC.
USA

ART DIRECTORS
DAVID SLACK
RYAN GAGNARD
DESIGNER
RYAN GAGNARD
CLIENT
KIMARK

context

context

1 Mount Stuart
West Bute Stree
Cardiff Bay
CF10 5BB
Wales, UK

t: +44 (0)29 2047 07
m: +44 (0)77 6039 883
f: +44 (0)870 831 6687

info@contextile.co.uk
www.contextile.co.uk

371
ELFEN
UNITED KINGDOM
DESIGNER
MATTHEW JAMES
CLIENT
CONTEXT
PAPER/MATERIALS
CYCLUS OFFSET

Faces Make-up Studio & Bridal Boutique
Faces Esthetic & Beauty Spa

155 East Beaver Creek Rd., Unit 21-22
Richmond Hill, Ontario L4B 2N1
www.facescanada.com

顏妝

Candy Tong

Faces Esthetic & Beauty Spa
phone. 905.763.7785

Faces Make-up Studio & Bridal Boutique
Faces Esthetic & Beauty Spa

155 East Beaver Creek Rd., Unit 21-22
Richmond Hill, Ontario L4B 2N1
www.facescanada.com

顏妝

Faces Make-up Studio & Bridal Boutique
Faces Esthetic & Beauty Spa

Jackie Lu

155 East Beaver Creek Rd., Unit 21-22
Richmond Hill, Ontario L4B 2N1
www.facescanada.com

顏妝

Faces Esthetic & Beauty Spa
phone. 905.763.7785

Sammie Liang

Faces Esthetic & Beauty Spa
phone. 905.763.7785

372
SPLASH INTERACTIVE LIMITED
CANADA
ART DIRECTOR
IVY WONG
DESIGNER
IVY WONG
CLIENT
FACES BRIDLE BOUTIQUE AND BEAUTY SPA
PAPER/MATERIALS
EUROSILK
DEBOSS
FOIL

373

EGG CREATIVES
SINGAPORE

ART DIRECTOR
JASON CHEN

DESIGNER
JASON CHEN

CLIENT
BOHEMIAN BUTTERFLY

PAPER/MATERIALS
260 GSM GLOSS ART

Visit our push-carts at:
Raffles City Level 2
& Centrepoint Level 1

Contact us at:
T 65 6559 9673
F 65 6245 8554
info@bohemianbutterfly.com.sg

www.**bohemianbutterfly**.com.sg

MAYHEM MEDIA
THE CREATIVE POWERPLANT
30 AMP 240 V.AC MAX. HP 7.5

CONTACT: ERIC HINES
FUSE: ERIC@MAYHEMMEDIA.COM
SERIAL #: 66.96.131.37

374

MAYHEM MEDIA
USA

DESIGNER
ERIC HINES

CLIENT
MAYHEM MEDIA

PAPER/MATERIALS
160# CLASSIC CREST

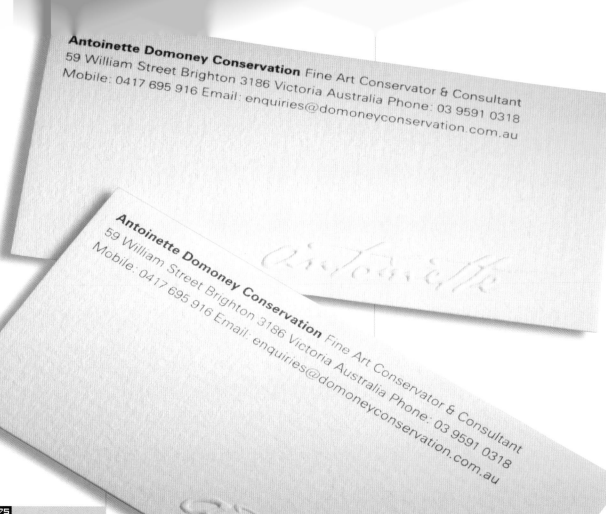

Antoinette Domoney Conservation Fine Art Conservator & Consultant
59 William Street Brighton 3186 Victoria Australia Phone: 03 9591 0318
Mobile: 0417 695 916 Email: enquiries@domoneyconservation.com.au

Antoinette Domoney Conservation Fine Art Conservator & Consultant
59 William Street Brighton 3186 Victoria Australia Phone: 03 9591 0318
Mobile: 0417 695 916 Email: enquiries@domoneyconservation.com.au

375

OCTAVO
AUSTRALIA
ART DIRECTOR
GARY DOMONEY
CLIENT
ANTOINETTE DOMONEY CONSERVATION
PAPER/MATERIALS
280 GSM CONSERVATION
ICE WHITE HESSIAN (RALEIGH PAPER)

376

BLOK DESIGN
MEXICO
ART DIRECTOR
VANESSA ECKSTEIN
DESIGNERS
VANESSA ECKSTEIN
VANESSA ENRIQUEZ
CLIENT
TALLER DE EMPRESA
PAPER/MATERIALS
STRATHMORE ULTIMATE WHITE

taller de empresa

rubén darío 281 p.18, polanco   tel : (52.55) 10.87.51.60
cp.11580, méxico df, méxico   fax : (52.55) 10.87.51.61

t→e

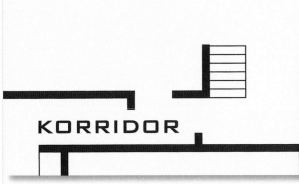

KORRIDOR

377
804© GRAPHIC DESIGN
GERMANY

ART DIRECTORS
**HELGE RIEDER
OLIVER HENN**

DESIGNERS
**HELGE RIEDER
OLIVER HENN**

CLIENT
**KORRIDOR GBR ARCHITEKTUR &
STADTPLANUNG**

PAPER/MATERIALS
**RÖMERTURM COLAMBO
GLETSCHER MATTE**

ARCHITEKTUR & STADTPLANUNG   **UTE MÖHRING**

BÖCKLINSTRASSE 22   D-40235 DÜSSELDORF
T: +49(0)211. 38 11 54   F: +49(0)211. 968 33 39
INFO@BUEROKORRIDOR.DE

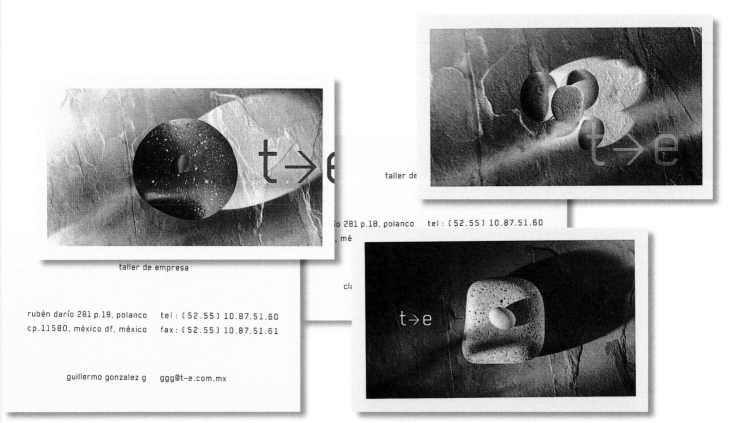

taller de empresa

rubén darío 281 p.18, polanco   tel : (52.55) 10.87.51.60
cp.11580, méxico df, méxico   fax : (52.55) 10.87.51.61

guillermo gonzalez g   ggg@t-e.com.mx

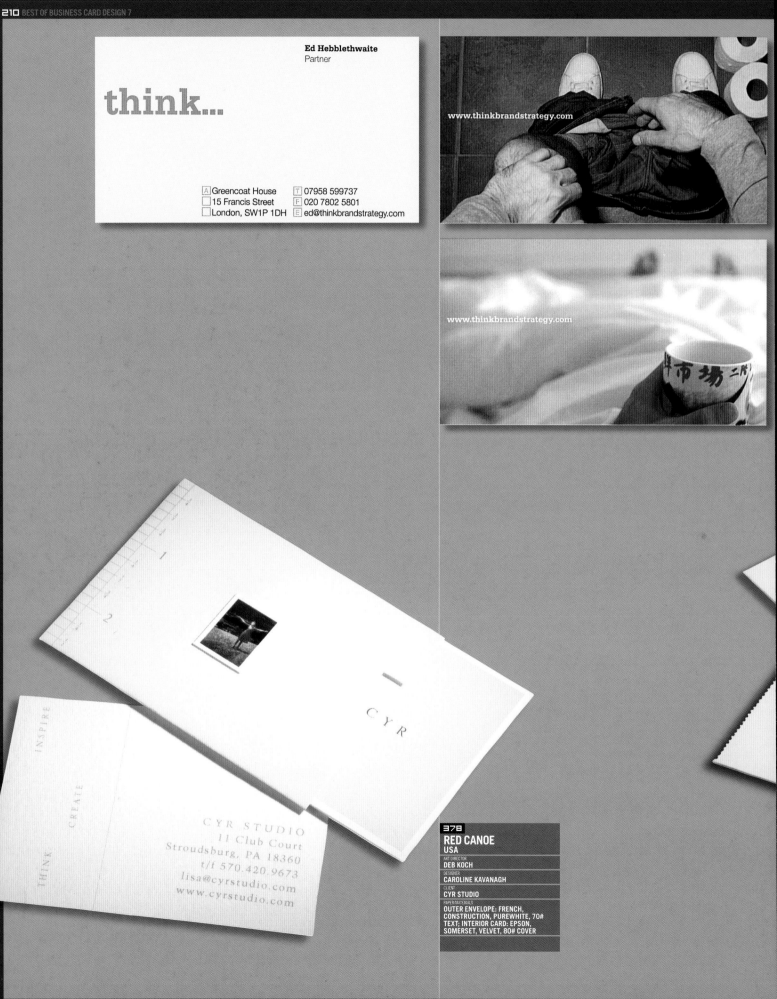

Ed Hebblethwaite
Partner

think...

[A] Greencoat House [T] 07958 599737
[ ] 15 Francis Street [F] 020 7802 5801
[ ] London, SW1P 1DH [E] ed@thinkbrandstrategy.com

www.thinkbrandstrategy.com

www.thinkbrandstrategy.com

CYR

CYR STUDIO
11 Club Court
Stroudsburg, PA 18360
t/f 570.420.9673
lisa@cyrstudio.com
www.cyrstudio.com

INSPIRE

CREATE

THINK

378
RED CANOE
USA
ART DIRECTOR
DEB KOCH
DESIGNER
CAROLINE KAVANAGH
CLIENT
CYR STUDIO
PAPER/MATERIALS
**OUTER ENVELOPE: FRENCH,
CONSTRUCTION, PUREWHITE, 70#
TEXT; INTERIOR CARD: EPSON,
SOMERSET, VELVET, 80# COVER**

379
THINK... BRAND STRATEGY
UNITED KINGDOM
ART DIRECTOR
STUART WOOD
DESIGNER
STUART WOOD
CLIENT
THINK... BRAND STRATEGY
PAPER/MATERIALS
WHITE MATTE ART

380
BONBON LONDON
UNITED KINGDOM
ART DIRECTOR
MARK HARPER
DESIGNER
MARK HARPER
CLIENT
MARK HARPER
PAPER/MATERIALS
SIMWHITE BOARD 450 MICRON

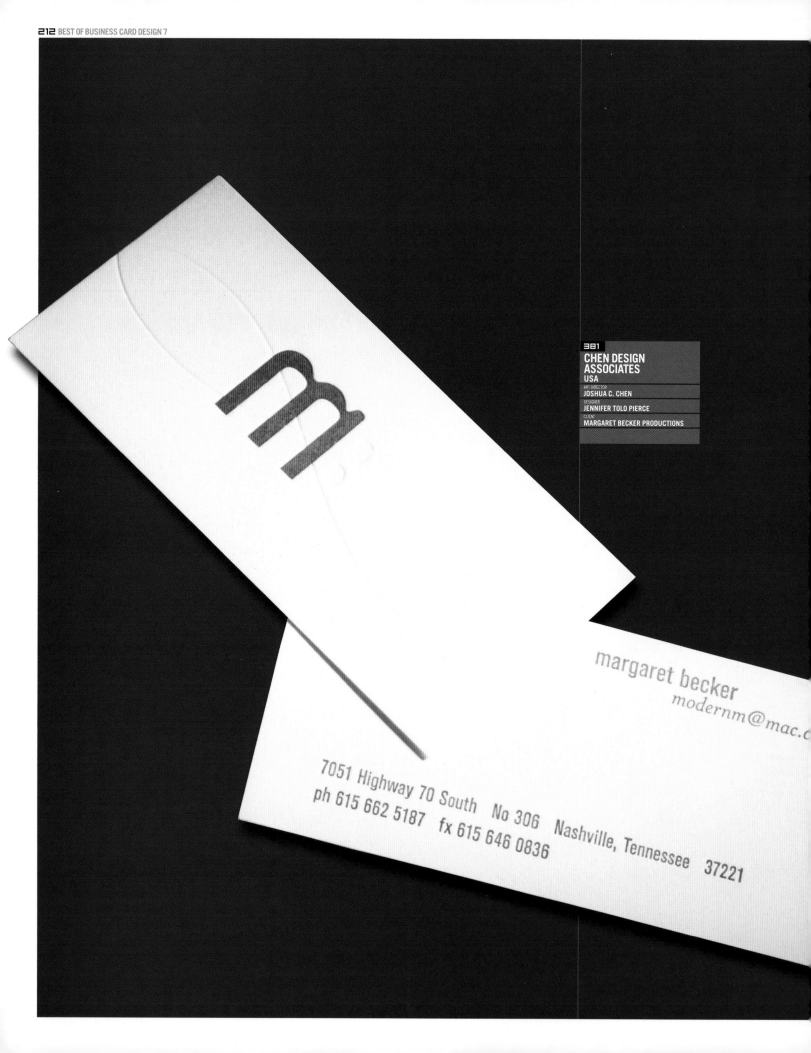

381
**CHEN DESIGN
ASSOCIATES**
USA
ART DIRECTOR
JOSHUA C. CHEN
DESIGNER
JENNIFER TOLO PIERCE
CLIENT
MARGARET BECKER PRODUCTIONS

margaret becker
modernm@mac.c

7051 Highway 70 South   No 306   Nashville, Tennessee   37221
ph 615 662 5187   fx 615 646 0836

Lynne Eccleston
Director

Rhea Consulting Pte Ltd
11 Collyer Quay #10-04
The Arcade
Singapore 049317
Tel +44 (0) 795 028 7235
Fax +65 6733 1102
lynne@rheaconsulting.com
www.rheaconsulting.com

transforming your business

382
EGG CREATIVES
SINGAPORE
ART DIRECTOR
JASON CHEN
DESIGNER
JASON CHEN
CLIENT
RHEA CONSULTING PTE LTD
PAPER/MATERIALS
260 GSM ART CARD
MATTE LAMINATE

383
WOLKEN COMMUNICA
USA
ART DIRECTOR
KURT WOLKEN
DESIGNER
GRETCHEN BJORK
CLIENT
WOLKEN COMMUNICA

julie schneider
julie@wolkencommunica.com

telephone 206 545.1696
facsimile 206 784.0989

2562 dexter ave north
seattle wa 98109

wolken communica

Darshan Singh Bhuller
Artistic Director
dsb@phoenixdancetheatre.co.uk

3 St Peter's Buildings
St Peter's Square
Leeds LS9 8AH England

Tel: 0113 242 3486
Fax: 0113 244 4736
www.phoenixdancetheatre.co.uk

384
THOMPSON
UNITED KINGDOM

ART DIRECTOR
IAN THOMPSON
DESIGNER
IAN THOMPSON
CLIENT
PHOENIX DANCE THEATRE
PAPER/MATERIALS
**CONQUEROR DIAMOND WHITE CX22
300 GSM**

CHRIS EVANS
SEVANS DESIGN

SEVANSDESIGN@MAIL.COM
434 E 73RD STREET   KANSAS CITY MO 64131
PH 816 237 1060   CELL 816 830 5077

386
SEVANS DESIGN
USA
DESIGNER
CHRIS EVANS
CLIENT
SEVANS DESIGN
PAPER/MATERIALS
3/1 WITH DIE CUT

385
**COMPLEXUS
ARCHITECTURE
AND DESIGN**
BRAZIL
ART DIRECTOR
RENATA LA ROCCA
DESIGNER
CLARISSA RIBEIRO
CLIENT
**COMPLEXUS ARCHITECTURE
AND DESIGN**
PAPER/MATERIALS
**PAPER: COUCHÉ 230 GSM
FILM: DULL
VARNISH: U.V.**

complexus

renata la rocca
arquiteta

complexus
arquitetura e design
rlr@complexus.com.br
[19]9153_6815

www.complexus.com.br

東西
EDX INTERNATIONAL

SINGAPORE HONG KONG · PARIS · LONDON · NEW YORK

387
EGG CREATIVES
SINGAPORE
ART DIRECTOR
JASON CHEN
DESIGNER
JASON CHEN
CLIENT
EDX INTERNATIONAL INCORPORATED
PAPER/MATERIALS
260 GSM RIVES DESIGN BRIGHT WHITE

Vivian Sim

EDX INTERNATIONAL INCORPORATED
Hong Kong Office
Rm 1006, 10F, New World Tower 1,
18 Queen's Road, Central, Hong Kong
Singapore Office
Tanglin Post Office PO Box 641
Singapore 912422
Mobile 852 977 18498
Email   vsim@edxint.com

388
FFURIOUS
SINGAPORE
ART DIRECTOR
LITTLE ONG
DESIGNER
LITTLE ONG
CLIENT
MARK LAPWOOD
PAPER/MATERIALS
250 GSM EAGLE SILHOUETTE
PREMIUM MATTE CARD
EMBOSSING

Mark cinematographer
Lapwood
phone au +61 410 586 776
email mark@marklapwood.com
web www.marklapwood.com

389
MUGGIE RAMADANI
DESIGN STUDIO
DENMARK
ART DIRECTOR
MUGGIE RAMADANI
DESIGNERS
MUGGIE RAMADANI
CLAUS RYSSER
CLIENT
ELI DIGITAL IMAGING

ELI LAJBOSCHITZ
DIGITAL IMAGING

STURLASGADE 12 L
DK-2300 COPENHAGEN S

P 0045 / 32 54 36 36
M 0045 / 26 34 26 28

E ELI@LEIBO.DK
W WWW.LEIBO.DK

ng +65 9096 1975
thai +66 12 977 959
viet +84 918 010 458
phil +63 927 590 3394

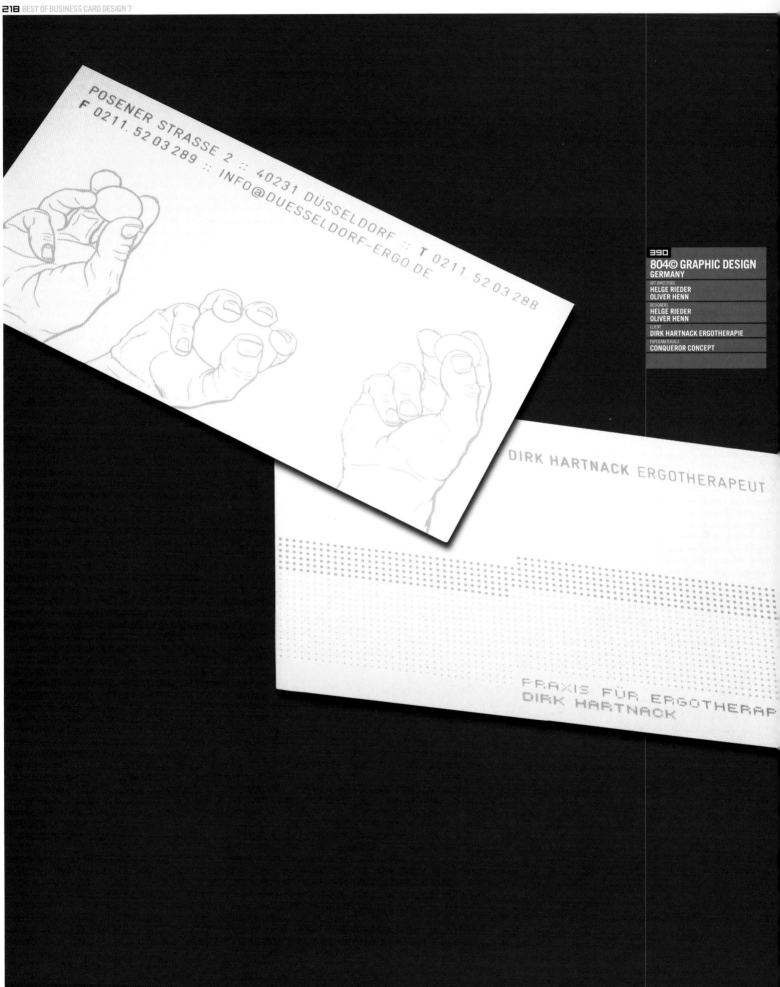

POSENER STRASSE 2 :: 40231 DÜSSELDORF :: **T** 0211.52 03 288
F 0211.52 03 289 :: INFO@DUESSELDORF-ERGO.DE

DIRK HARTNACK ERGOTHERAPEUT

PRAXIS FÜR ERGOTHERAP
DIRK HARTNACK

390

804© GRAPHIC DESIGN
GERMANY
ART DIRECTORS
HELGE RIEDER
OLIVER HENN
DESIGNERS
HELGE RIEDER
OLIVER HENN
CLIENT
DIRK HARTNACK ERGOTHERAPIE
PAPER/MATERIALS
CONQUEROR CONCEPT

PïnK

business interiors

HAWORTH

JOE DONDELINGER
Business Development

5825 EXCELSIOR BLVD
MINNEAPOLIS MN 55416
T 952.915.3104
F 952.915.3121
1.800.342.7990
joe.dondelinger@pinkbi.com

SPACE PLANNING

FACILITY SERVICES

FURNISHINGS

391
CAPSULE
USA
ART DIRECTOR
BRIAN ADDUCCI
CLIENT
THE PUSH INSTITUTE
PAPER/MATERIALS
PINK BUSINESS INTERIORS

392
**OXYGEN DESIGN +
COMMUNICATIONS**
CANADA
ART DIRECTOR
ALEX WIGINGTON
DESIGNER
ALEX WIGINGTON
CLIENT
OXYGEN SPACE INC.
PAPER/MATERIALS
MOHAWK SUPERFINE

OXYGEN SPACE

Alex Wigington
PRINCIPAL

401 Richmond St W, Suite 430   t 416 506 0₂0₂ x27
Toronto, ON M5V 3A8   f 416 506 170₂
oxygen.ca   alex@oxygen.ca

MOE
SIZE L

DO NOT MACHINE WASH OR TUMBLE DRY!!!
DO NOT FILL WITH RAKIJA
IN CASE OF CROATIAN LANGUAGE, MIGHT ACT CONFUSED
FUNCTIONS SLOWER AT BELOW FREEZING TEMPERATURES
DO NOT ALLOW TO SING
FREQUENT HYPERACTIVITY MIGHT OCCUR

100% CREATIVE
MADE IN LEBANON

@SHOPPING IS NOT A CRIME

HELP ME TO HELP Y

BRUKETA&ŽINIĆ OM
MILJANA DRAGIČEVIĆ+POSLOVNA TAJNICA
ZAVRTNICA 17, 10 000 ZAGREB, CROATIA
T: + 385 1 6064 000, F: + 385 1 6064 001, M: + 385 98 98 323 80
MILJANA@BRUKETA-ZINIC.COM, WWW.BRUKETA-ZINIC.COM

Lakemont Village
4053 Lakemont Blvd. SE #84, Bellevue, Washington 98006
T 425 865 9400, F 425 865 9565, www.motivodesign.com

motivo

393
BRUKETA & ZINIC
CROATIA
ART DIRECTOR
SINISA SUDAR
DESIGNER
SINISA SUDAR
CLIENT
BRUKETA & ZINIC
PAPER/MATERIALS
LAKE EXTRA 350

394
WOLKEN COMMUNICA
USA
ART DIRECTOR
KURT WOLKEN
CLIENT
MOTIVO

396

SONSOLES LLORENS
SPAIN

ART DIRECTOR
SONSOLES LLORENS

DESIGNER
SONSOLES LLORENS

CLIENT
RAFAEL VARGAS

RAFAEL VARGAS
FOTOGRAFIA

GRAN VIA CORTS CATALANES 699 1ER 1A · E-08013 BARCELONA
TEL (34) 93 246 36 02 · FAX (34) 93 232 41 51

312 2170734

312 2170734

BEN

395

FUNNEL
USA

DESIGNER
ERIC KASS

CLIENT
FORGET COMPUTERS

PAPER/MATERIALS
PLASTIC

www.skbarchitects.com

397
WOLKEN COMMUNICA
USA
ART DIRECTOR
KURT WOLKEN
DESIGNER
KURT WOLKEN
CLIENT
SKB ARCHITECTS

SkB
ARCHITECTS
Olivia Ireland
designer
oireland@skbarchitects.com

1525 First Avenue #7A Seattle WA 98101
P 206 903 0575 F 206 903 1586

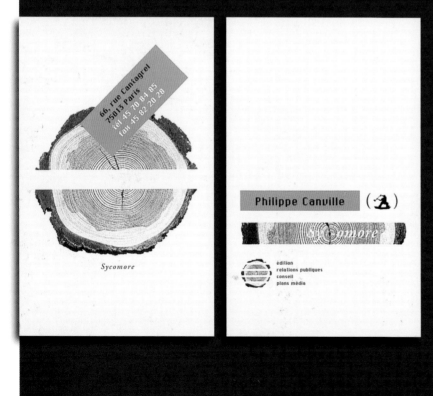

66, rue Cantagrel
75013 Paris
tél 45 70 84 85
fax 45 82 20 28

Sycomore

Philippe Canville ( )

Sycomore

édition
relations publiques
conseil
plans média

398
FABRICE PRAEGER
FRANCE
ART DIRECTOR
FABRICE PRAEGER
DESIGNER
FABRICE PRAEGER
CLIENT
SYCOMORE
PAPER/MATERIALS
COATED

⇨ **THE PUSH INSTITUTE**
420 NORTH FIFTH STREET
SUITE 645
MINNEAPOLIS, MN 55401

⇨ **CECILY SOMMERS**
FOUNDER & PRESIDENT

⇨ CSOMMERS@PUSHTHEFU⁻
612.374.3191_PH
612.377.0611 F⁻

...URE IN NEW DIRECTIONS

...UTURE.ORG

PUSH

...ITUTE
...TH STREET

...N 55401

⇨ **CECILY SOMMERS**
FOUNDER & PRESIDENT

⇨ CSOMMERS@PUSHTHEFUTURE.ORG
612.374.3191_PH
612.377.0611_FX

...TE
...STREET

...MN 55401

⇨ **CECILY SOMMERS**
FOUNDER & PRESIDENT

⇨ CSOMMERS@PUSHTHEFU...
612.374.3191_PH
612.377.0611_FX

399
CAPSULE
USA
ART DIRECTOR
BRIAN ADDUCCI
DESIGNER
GREG BROSE
CLIENT
THE PUSH INSTITUTE
PAPER/MATERIALS
FIBERMARK HALFTONE PRINTABLE

400
ATELIER WORKS
UNITED KINGDOM
ART DIRECTOR
IAN CHILVERS
DESIGNER
JOSEPH LUFFMAN
CLIENT
ROYAL GEOGRAPHICAL SOCIETY
(WITH IBG)
PAPER/MATERIALS
300 GSM PRINTSPEED

51°45'.17 N, 1°15'.19 W

Ed Badger born in Oxford, England

28°37'N, 77°13'E

Rinku Mitra born in New Delhi, India

Robbye Harrill
IT Manager

1 Kensington Gore
London SW7 2AR

T +44 (0)20 7591 3039
F +44 (0)20 7591 3001
E r.harrill@rgs.org
W www.rgs.org

Royal
Geographical
Society
with IBG

Advancing geography
and geographical learning

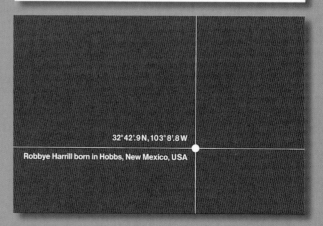

32°42'.9 N, 103°8'.8 W

Robbye Harrill born in Hobbs, New Mexico, USA

rauter > o 323+934+9106 > f 323+937+0550 > m 310+500+7987

e@triagefilms.com > 145 5

TRIAGE ⚡

402
GEYRHALTER DESIGN
USA

ART DIRECTOR
FABIAN GEYRHALTER

DESIGNER
FABIAN GEYRHALTER

CLIENT
TRIAGE

PAPER/MATERIALS
MCCOY

UGGIE RAMADANI DESIGN STUDIO

eramadani.com, www.muggieramadani.com

401
MUGGIE RAMADANI
DESIGN STUDIO
DENMARK

ART DIRECTOR
MUGGIE RAMADANI

DESIGNER
MUGGIE RAMADANI

CLIENT
MUGGIE RAMADANI DESIGN STUDIO

Coverall
CUSTOM UPHOLSTERY
FOR ANY SPACE

CARL NICHOLS
MASTER UPHOLSTERER

☐ HOME
☐ AUTO
☐ MARINE
☐ **AIRCRAFT**

A sewing machine. Some thread.
And a little imagination. At Coverall,
we'll transform any space with
custom upholstery. Whether it's
an entire room or a single window
treatment, we'll work with you every
step of the way. Our commitment
to customer satisfaction is based
on one simple idea: the golden rule.
Ask us about it and discover
what all the fuss is about.

706 LAKESIDE AVENUE MCCALL IDAHO 83638

AREA CODE
NO. 208

MADE IN U.S.A.

P : 634.6661

IDRISI

403
Q
GERMANY
ART DIRECTOR
THILO VON DEBSCHITZ
DESIGNER
MARCEL KUMMERER
CLIENT
IDRISI

404
FUNNEL
USA
DESIGNER
ERIC KASS
CLIENT
CARL NICHOLS / COVERALL
PAPER/MATERIALS
CANVAS

404
FUNNEL
USA
DESIGNER
ERIC KASS
CLIENT
CARL NICHOLS / COVERALL
PAPER/MATERIALS
CANVAS

406
SONSOLES LLORENS
SPAIN
ART DIRECTOR
SONSOLES LLORENS
DESIGNER
SONSOLES LLORENS
CLIENT
NEGRO

BAR RESTAURANT COPES
AV DIAGONAL 640 EDIFICI CAJA MADRID 08017 BARCELONA
T 934 059 444 F 934 059 221

Gamzu Neumark Ltd.
diamond manufacturers

405
TAMAR MANY AND YANEK IONTEF
ISRAEL
ART DIRECTORS
TAMAR MANY
YANEK IONTEF
DESIGNERS
TAMAR MANY
YANEK IONTEF
CLIENT
GAMZU NEWMARK LTD
PAPER/MATERIALS
OFFSET PRINTING ON COATED PAPER

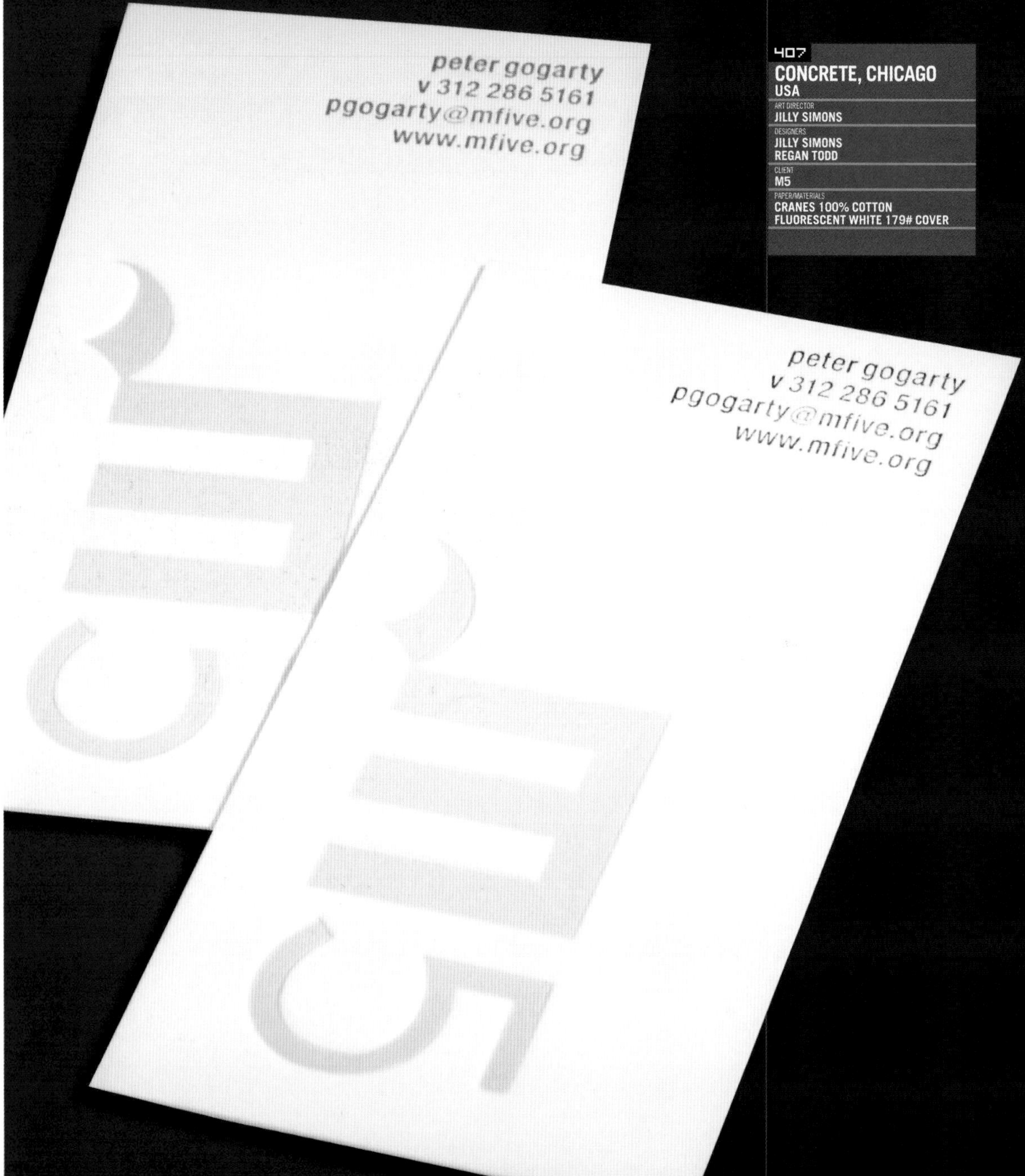

peter gogarty
v 312 286 5161
pgogarty@mfive.org
www.mfive.org

peter gogarty
v 312 286 5161
pgogarty@mfive.org
www.mfive.org

407
CONCRETE, CHICAGO
USA
ART DIRECTOR
JILLY SIMONS
DESIGNERS
JILLY SIMONS
REGAN TODD
CLIENT
M5
PAPER/MATERIALS
CRANES 100% COTTON
FLUORESCENT WHITE 179# COVER

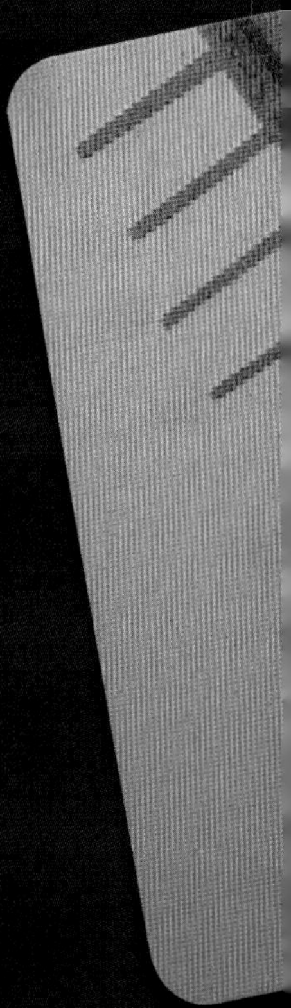

408
ISOTOPE 221
USA
ART DIRECTOR
CHRISTOPHER CANNON
DESIGNERS
DORIT KRIESLER
DAVID SANTUS
CLIENT
URBAN MAPPING LLC
PAPER/MATERIALS
LENTICULAR PRINTING
PLASTIC LENS ADHERED TO PAPER

UrbanMapping

Ian White
ian@urbanmapping.com

545 Eighth Avenue
Suite 401
New York, NY 10018

Tel 212.242.8267
Fax 212.937.3578
866.DYNAMAP

www.urbanmapping.com

NEW YORK
UNIVERSITY

GUGGENHEIM
MUSEUM SOHO

SOHO

Photography

旗手浩

151-0071 東京都渋谷区本町 1-10-1-401

Tel&Fax 03-3378-6012

Mobile 080-5089-4476

ydncm601@ybb.ne.jp

Hatate Hiroshi
1-10-1-401 Honmachi, Shibuyaku
Tokyo 151-0071 Japan

409
V06
BRAZIL
ART DIRECTOR
YOMAR AUGUSTO
DESIGNER
YOMAR AUGUSTO
CLIENT
HATATE HIROSHI

CRACKS FRESH IDEAS.

EGGCREATIVES.COM

411

EGG CREATIVES
SINGAPORE
ART DIRECTOR
JASON CHEN
DESIGNER
JASON CHEN
CLIENT
EGG CREATIVES
PAPER/MATERIALS
310 GSM ART CARD GLOSS LAMINTATE

LIM CHOON PIN · CONSULTANT

EGG·CREATIVES

12 EAN KIAM PLACE SINGAPORE 429109
T 6339 1413 **F** 6339 1418 **M** 9694 7382
DESIGN@EGGCREATIVES.COM

fuel for your IT solution

tsai jen yang
director

your mailing address here
(O) 1234 5678
(F) 1234 5678
(M) 1234 5678
(E) jenyang@ft.com

www.**fueltech**.com

410

EGG CREATIVES
SINGAPORE
ART DIRECTOR
LIM CHOON PIN
DESIGNER
LIM CHOON PIN
CLIENT
FUEL TECH
PAPER/MATERIALS
260 GSM ART CARD
MATTE LAMINATE

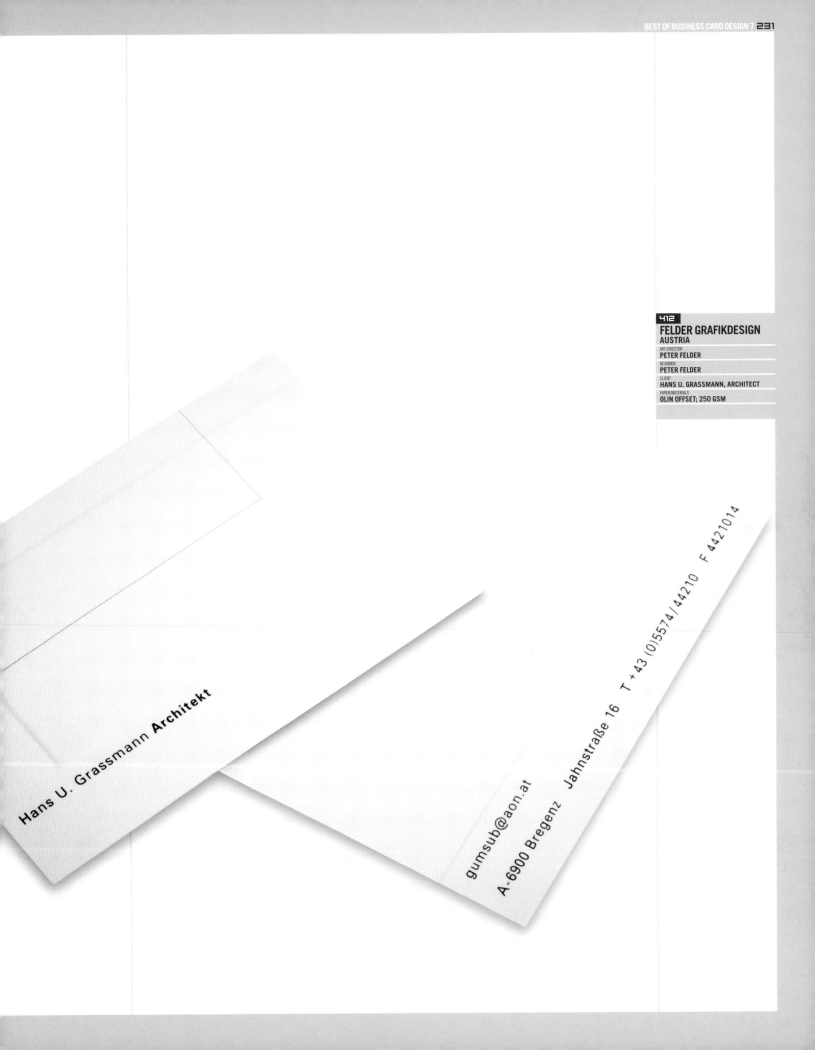

412
FELDER GRAFIKDESIGN
AUSTRIA
ART DIRECTOR
PETER FELDER
DESIGNER
PETER FELDER
CLIENT
HANS U. GRASSMANN, ARCHITECT
PAPER/MATERIALS
OLIN OFFSET; 250 GSM

Hans U. Grassmann **Architekt**

gumsub@aon.at

A-6900 Bregenz Jahnstraße 16 T +43 (0)5574/44210 F 4421014

P 612
339
3039

F 612
333
2278

W fifth
street
net

danwest
danefifthstreet.net

5

fifthstreet
DESIGN/WEB/PRINT

1018 fifth str
minneapolis
55411 us

NAME: Raphael Pohlan

EMAIL: pohland@stilradar.de

stilradar visual resources   Schwabstr. 10 a   70197 Stut

T 0711 887 55 20   F 0711 882 23 44   M 0172 73

stilradar

DIRECTORY

> PROMPTT
49 MISSOURI STREET #10
SAN FRANCISCO, CA 94107
U.S.A.
415.431.4173
CORRINE@PROMPTT.COM
(174)

300MILLION
1 ROSOMAN PLACE, EXMOUTH MARKET
LONDON EC1R 0JY
UNITED KINGDOM
+44 20.7833.3838
CHRIS@300MILLION.COM
(21, 69)

32BITS™ DESIGN EM MULTIMEIOS
AV. RIO BRANCO 257 / 908
CENTRO, RIO DE JANEIRO, RJ 20040-009
BRAZIL
+55 21.9101.5533
DANIELMORENA@32BITS.COM.BR
(180)

3RD EDGE COMMUNICATIONS
162 NEWARK AVENUE
JERSEY CITY, NJ 07302
U.S.A.
201.395.9960
ROB@3RDEDGE.COM
(70, 147, 253)

804© GRAPHIC DESIGN
RONSDORFER STRASSE 77A
40233 DÜSSELDORF
GERMANY
+49 211.77.92.76.0
INFO@ACHTNULLVIER.DE
(136, 330, 377, 390)

9MYLES, INC.
2817 TURNBULL STREET
OCEANSIDE, CA 92054
U.S.A.
858.344.8619
FUEL@9MYLES.COM
(66, 116, 128, 158, 212)

A3 DESIGN
7809 CAUSEWAY DRIVE, SUITE 207
CHARLOTTE, NC 28227
U.S.A.
704.568.5351
ALAN@ATHREEDESIGN.COM
(50, 206)

ALOOF DESIGN
5 FISHER STREET, LEWES
E. SUSSEX BN7 2DG
UNITED KINGDOM
+44 1273.470887
MICHELLE@ALOOFDESIGN.COM
(184)

ALR DESIGN
2701 EDGEWOOD AVENUE
RICHMOND, VA 23222
U.S.A.
804.321.6677
CONTACT@ALRDESIGN.COM
(134, 218)

ARKKIT FORMS
692A MOULTON AVENUE
LOS ANGELES, CA 90031
U.S.A.
323.227.0191
ARKKIT@PACBELL.NET
(322)

ATELIER WORKS
THE OLD PIANO FACTORY, 5 CHARLTON KINGS ROAD
LONDON NW5 2SB
UNITED KINGDOM
+44 20.7284.2215
IAN@ATELIERWORKS.CO.UK
(16, 400)

AUFULDISH & WARINNER
183 THE ALAMEDA
SAN ANSELMO, CA 94960
U.S.A.
415.721.7921
BOB@AUFWAR.COM
(291)

JAN BARKER AND DAVID CAUNCE
67 ACRES ROAD, CHORLTON
MANCHESTER M21 9GB
UNITED KINGDOM
+44 161.861.9309
JAN@CONNECTPOINT.CO.UK
(133)

BASE ART CO.
623 HIGH STREET
WORTHINGTON, OH 43085
U.S.A.
614.841.7480
TBACH@BASEARTCO.COM
(57, 274, 353)

BAWIDAMANN DESIGN INC.
1549 NORTHWEST BOULEVARD
COLUMBUS, OH 43212
U.S.A.
614.323.0401
ANDREW@BAWIDAMANN.COM
(214)

BECKER DESIGN
225 E. ST. PAUL AVENUE, SUITE 300
MILWAUKEE, WI 53202
414.224.4942
STEPHEN@BECKERDESIGN.NET
(223)

BELL SPORTS
380 ENCINAL STREET
SANTA CRUZ, CA 95060
831.420.4070
CPOTTER@BELLSPORTS.COM
(237)

BLIK
655 G STREET, SUITE E
SAN DIEGO, CA 92101
U.S.A.
619.234.4434
TYLER@TYLERBLIK.COM
(17)

BLOK DESIGN
AVE. MEXICO 85 #1
LA CONDESA 06100
MEXICO, D.F.
MEXICO
+52 55.55.53.5076
BLOKDESIGN@ATT.NET.MX
(91, 104, 135, 179, 195, 225, 269, 376)

BLUEROOM
SAGVEIEN 21A
0459 OSLO
NORWAY
+47 909.60831
CONTACT@BLUEROOM.NO
(258, 260, 263, 272)

BLUESHAPE
274 HAKALAU PLACE
HONOLULU, HI 96825
U.S.A.
808.554.5005
DEREK@BLUESHAPE.COM
(233)

BOCCALATTE
P.O. BOX 370
SURRY HILLS, SYDNEY, NSW 2010
AUSTRALIA
+61 2.9310.4149
INFO@BOCCALATTE.COM
(151)

BONBON LONDON
F5
13 THE PARAGON
LONDON SE3 0PA
UNITED KINGDOM
+44 20.8297.4240
MARK@BONBONLONDON.COM
(348, 380)

BRUKETA & ZINIC
ZAVRTNICA 17
ZAGREB 10 000
CROATIA
+385 1.6064.000
BRUKETA-ZINIC@BRUKETA-ZINIC.COM
(228, 393)

BUCHANAN DESIGN
5230 CARROLL CANYON ROAD #226
SAN DIEGO, CA 92121
U.S.A.
858.450.1150
BOBBY@BUCHANANDESIGN.COM
(153, 338)

BUNGEE ASSOCIATES
804A NORTH BRIDGE ROAD
SINGAPORE 198772
SINGAPORE
+65 6299.5983
JOE@BUNGEEASSOCIATES.COM
(196)

BÜROGRAFIC
HATTINGERSTRASSE 764
44879 BOCHUM
GERMANY
+49 234.338.6280
TIM@BUEROGRAFIC.COM
(282, 303)

CAMPBELL FISHER DESIGN
3333 EAST CAMELBACK ROAD, SUITE 200
PHOENIX, AZ 85018
U.S.A.
602.955.2707
SC@THINKCFD.COM
(142, 221, 268, 294, 324)

CAPSULE
10 S. FIFTH STREET #645
MINNEAPOLIS, MN 55402
U.S.A.
612.341.4525
GEGBERT@CAPSULE.US
(273, 354, 355, 391, 399)

CHEN DESIGN ASSOCIATES
589 HOWARD STREET, 4TH FLOOR
SAN FRANCISCO, CA 94105
U.S.A.
415.896.5338
INFO@CHENDESIGN.COM
(346, 359, 381)

CHRISTIANSEN: CREATIVE
P.O. BOX 1022
HUDSON, WI 54016
U.S.A.
715.381.8480
TRICIA@CHRISTIANSENCREATIVE.COM
(318)

CIRCLE K STUDIO
300 BRANNAN STREET, SUITE 308
SAN FRANCISCO, CA 94107
U.S.A.
415.243.0606
JULIE@CIRCLEKSTUDIO.COM
(165, 168, 344, 368)

COMPLEXUS ARCHITECTURE AND DESIGN
RUA JOANÓPOLIS
NO. 130 – JD. ADÉLIA
SANTA BÁRBARA D'OESTE, SÃO PAULO
BRAZIL
+55 19.9153.6815
COMPLEXUS@COMPLEXUS.COM.BR
(347, 385)

CONCRETE, CHICAGO
407 S. DEARBORN STREET, SUITE 230
CHICAGO, IL 60605
U.S.A.
312.427.3733
JILLY@CONCRETE-US.COM
(254, 356, 407)

CUSP DESIGN
11 VILLAGE STREET #2
SOMERVILLE, MA 02143
U.S.A.
617.623.8065
DOLIVER@CUSPDESIGN.COM
(320)

D-FUSE
13–14 ST. SUTTON STREET
LONDON EC1V 0BX
UNITED KINGDOM
+44 20.7253.3462
MIKE@DFUSE.COM
(218)

DAL BELLO
RUA ALVARES DE AZEVEDO 147 / 1001
RJ 24220-020
BRAZIL
+55 21.2709.5897
REJANE@DALBELLO.COM
(43)

DANIELLE FOUSHÉE DESIGN
10865 BLUFFSIDE DRIVE #308
STUDIO CITY, CA 91204
U.S.A.
818.613.7459
DANIELLE@DANIELLEFOUSHEE.COM
(105)

DEMIURGE UNIT
401 EAST 34TH STREET #N11J
NEW YORK, NY 10016
U.S.A.
212.725.1130
TEDDY@LEDARTIST.COM
(192)

DESIGN BY MILA
6250 HOLABIRD STREET, APT. B
SAN DIEGO, CA 92120
U.S.A.
619.920.0302
DESIGNBYMILA@YAHOO.COM
(15)

DESIGN NUT, LLC
3716 LAWRENCE AVENUE
KENSINGTON, MD 20895
U.S.A.
301.942.2360
BRENT@DESIGNNUT.COM
(232)

DESIGNKARMA INC.
P.O. BOX 1607
NEW YORK, NY 10028
U.S.A.
917.312.9973
INFO@DESIGNKARMA.COM
(103)

DIMAQUINA
RUA PACHECO LEÃO 704 CASA 21
JARDIM BOTÂNICO, RIO DE JANEIRO, RJ 22460-030
BRAZIL
+55 21.25296140
NAKO@DIMAQUINA.COM
(22, 235)

DIMENSI + GRAPHIC DESIGN
INDONESIA
(5, 59)

DULUDE
4623 HARVARD
MONTRÉAL, QC H4A 2X3,
CANADA
514.431.9735
DENIS@DULUDE.CA
(49, 183, 249)

EDESIGN MEDIA
10441 SCENIC CIRCLE
CUPERTINO, CA 95014
U.S.A.
408.202.1731
JUNGLEDOG@GMAIL.COM
(48)

EGG CREATIVES
12 EAN KIAM PLACE
SINGAPORE 429109
SINGAPORE
+65 6339.1413
DESIGN@EGGCREATIVES.COM
(314, 373, 382, 387, 410, 411)

EGGERS + DIAPER
HECKMANNUFER 6A
10997 BERLIN
GERMANY
+49 30.6951.8085
MD@EGGERS-DIAPER.COM
(111, 205, 288)

ELFEN
20 HARROWBY LANE
CARDIFF BAY CF10 5GN
WALES, UNITED KINGDOM
+44 29.2048.4824
GUTO@ELFEN.CO.UK
(198, 371)

EMERYFROST
LEVEL 1, 15 FOSTER STREET
SURRY HILLS, SYDNEY, NSW 2010
AUSTRALIA
+61 2.9280.4233
SHARON.NIXON@EMERYFROST.COM
(239)

ENLIGHTENMENT
3–16 KAMINOGE
SETAGAYA-KU
TOKYO 158-0093
JAPAN
+81 3.3705.5470
HS@ELM-ART.COM
(117)

ENTERMOTION DESIGN STUDIO
105 S. BROADWAY STREET, SUITE 800
WICHITA, KS 67202
U.S.A.
316.264.2277
INFO@ENTERMOTION.COM
(100, 171)

ENTERPRISE IG
THE DESIGN CENTRE
19 TAMBACH ROAD, SUNNINGHILL
JOHANNESBURG
SOUTH AFRICA
+27 11.319.8000
DAVE.HOLLAND@ENTERPRISE1G.CO.ZA
(299)

FELDER GRAFIKDESIGN
ALEMANNENSTRASSE 49
6830 RANKWEIL
AUSTRIA
+43 5522.45002
FELDER.GRAFIK@AON.AT
(227, 305, 367, 412)

FFURIOUS
32A SAGO STREET
SINGAPORE 059025
SINGAPORE
+65 6225.0887
LITTLE@FFURIOUS.COM
(42, 271, 345, 388)

FIFTH STREET DESIGN
SEE: WESTCARR DESIGN

FITCH, SEATTLE
1218 3RD AVENUE #620
SEATTLE, WA 98101
U.S.A.
206.624.0551
KIM_LUKENS@LEONHARDT-FITCH.COM
(20)

FRANK FORD
533 TWIN BRIDGES ROAD
ALEXANDRIA, LA 71303
U.S.A.
318.445.7631
IDEAS@FRANKFORD.COM
(189)

FREE ASSOCIATION
68 GREEN STREET #1
JAMAICA PLAIN, MA 02130
U.S.A.
617.913.2731
JASON@FREEASSOCIATION.US
(297)

FUNNEL: ERIC KASS: UTILITARIAN + COMMERCIAL + FINE: ART
1969 SPRUCE DRIVE
CARMEL, IN 46033
U.S.A.
317.590.5355
ERIC@FUNNEL.TV
(13, 149, 186, 204, 395, 404)

GABRIEL KALACH – GRAPHIC DESIGN
1000 WEST AVENUE #1004
MIAMI BEACH, FL 33139
U.S.A.
305.532.2336
PROARTGRAPHICS@MAC.COM
(277)

LIZETTE GECEL
4706 AUGUSTA AVENUE
RICHMOND, VA 23230
U.S.A.
804.359.1711
LIZETTEGECEL@VERIZON.NET
(244, 317)

GEYRHALTER DESIGN
2525 MAIN STREET, SUITE 205
SANTA MONICA, CA 90405
U.S.A.
310.392.7615
INFO@GEYRHALTER.COM
(24, 313, 402)

GIG DESIGN
P.O. BOX 1431
OAKDALE, CA 95361
U.S.A.
209.605.7028
LARIMIE@GIGSPOT.COM
(261, 358)

GIRASOLE
110 BANK STREET
SUITE 5K
NEW YORK, NY 10014
U.S.A.
201.953.4687
DANIELA@GIRASOLEDESIGNS.COM
(203)

GLITSCHKA STUDIOS
5165 SYCAN COURT SE
SALEM, OR 97306
U.S.A.
971.223.6143
INFO@GLITSCHKA.COM
(141)

GOUTHIER DESIGN
2604 NW 54TH STREET
FT. LAUDERDALE, FL 33309
U.S.A.
954.739.7430
KILEY@GOUTHIER.COM
(30, 307)

GRAFIK-KLUB
HUMBOLDTSTRASSE 38
44787 BOCHUM
GERMANY
+49 234.9117.1857
CONTACT@STEINERT-DESIGN.COM
(310)

GRAFIKSTUDIO-STEINERT
HUMBOLDTSTRASSE 38
44787 BOCHUM
GERMANY
+49 234.9117.1857
CONTACT@STEINERT-DESIGN.COM
(278)

GRAFIKZ
RUA PAMPLONA 33, CASA 3
SÃO PAULO, SP 01405-000
BRAZIL
+55 11.3171.2153
APOLESSI@GRAFIKZ.COM
(256, 270)

GRAPHICULTURE
322 1ST AVENUE N. #500
MINNEAPOLIS, MN 55401
U.S.A.
612.339.8271
JANICE.STANFORD@GRAPHICULTURE.COM
(279)

GRAPHISCHE FORMGEBUNG
PULVERSTRASSE 25
44869 BOCHUM
GERMANY
+49 23.27.95.76.21
HERBERT.ROHSIEPE@T-ONLINE.DE
(175, 300)

H
1055 ST. CHARLES AVENUE, SUITE 300
NEW ORLEANS, LA 70130
U.S.A.
504.522.6300
WINNIE@THINKH.COM
(309)

HAND MADE SRL
VIA SARTORI, 16
STIA (AR) 52017
ITALY
+39 575.582083
A.ESTERI@HMG.IT
(162, 259)

HARRIMANSTEEL
STUDIO 3.08, TEA BUILDING
56 SHOREDITCH HIGH STREET
LONDON E1 6JJ
UNITED KINGDOM
+44 20.7324.7530
JULIAN@HARRIMANSTEEL.CO.UK
(51, 81, 202, 262, 312)

HOCHSCHULE FÜR KÜNSTE BREMEN
UNIVERSITY OF THE ARTS BREMEN
AM SPEICHER XI 8
28217 BREMEN
GERMANY
+44 431.95.95.1391
AQUARIUM@HFK-BREMEN.DE
(231)

HORNALL ANDERSON DESIGN WORKS
1008 WESTERN AVENUE, SUITE 600
SEATTLE, WA 98104
U.S.A.
206.826.2329
C_ARBINI@HADW.COM
(207, 290, 325)

I_D BUERO GMBH
BISMARCKSTRASSE 67A
70197 STUTTGART
GERMANY
+49 711.636.8000
MAIL@I-DBUERO.DE
(54)

ICONTRACT
158, LAVELLE ROAD
BANGALORE 560001, KARNATAKA
INDIA
+91 80.22217015
COPYWRITER27@YAHOO.CO.UK
(58)

IMAGINE
THE STABLES, DUCIE STREET
MANCHESTER M1 2JN
UNITED KINGDOM
+44 161.272.8334
DAVID@IMAGINE-CGA.CO.UK
(97, 110, 155, 211)

INGALLS DESIGN
10 ARKANSAS STREET, SUITE E
SAN FRANCISCO, CA 94107
U.S.A.
415.626.6395
LINA@INGALLSDESIGN.COM
(217)

INKBYTE DESIGN
1851 NW 125TH AVENUE, SUITE 307
PEMBROKE PINES, FL 33028
U.S.A.
954.437.8588
PETER@INKBYTEDESIGN.COM
(106)

YANEK IONTEF
6 KESHET STREET #33
QIRYAT ONO 55401
ISRAEL
+972 3.5371476
YANEK@NETVISION.NET IL
(74, 301, 405)

ISOTOPE 221
232 WASHINGTON AVENUE, 4TH FLOOR
BROOKLYN, NY 11205
U.S.A.
718.783.3092
INFO@ISOTOPE221.COM
(352, 408)

JASON AND JASON
HAYETZIRA 11B
RAANANA 43663
ISRAEL
+972 9.7444282
TAMAR@JASONANDJASON.COM
(340)

JIM O'CONNOR COPYWRITING
THE WHITE COTTAGE, MUTTON LANE, WEDMORE
SOMERSET B5 28 4DS
UNITED KINGDOM
+44 1934.713154
WHITECOTTAGE1@BTINTERNET.COM
(8)

JOY DESIGN
1894 GILLIAN WAY
SAN JOSE, CA 95132
U.S.A.
408.202.4945
JYOUNG@JOYDESIGN.COM
(342)

KEARNEYROCHOLL
SCHWANTHALERSTRASSE 59A
60596 FRANKFURT
GERMANY
+49 69.606088.0
ROCHOLL@KEARNEYROCHOLL.DE
(2, 83, 240)

KESSELSKRAMER
LAURIERGRACHT 39
1016 RG AMSTERDAM
THE NETHERLANDS
+31 20.5301060
BUFFY@KESSELSKRAMER.COM
(28, 88, 130, 154, 245, 246, 364)

KINETIC SINGAPORE
2 LENG KEE ROAD
THYE HONG CENTRE
#04-03A SINGAPORE 159086
SINGAPORE
+65 6379.5320
RO@KINETIC.COM.SG
(4, 40, 45, 178, 242)

KISS&BAJS AB
BELLMANSGATAN 8
SE-118 20 STOCKHOLM
SWEDEN
+46 8.642.49.00
EMMA@PEEANDPOO.COM
(296)

KLOBODA
48 SPRINGHURST AVENUE
TORONTO, ON M6K 1B6
CANADA
416.534.7736
KAROLINA@KLOBODA.COM
(201)

KOMMUNIKATIONS-DESIGN
ELSENSTRASSE 31
40227 DÜSSELDORF
GERMANY
+49 211.7.333.290
MAIL@NINADAVID.DE
(44)

KONTRAPUNKT
KNEZOVA 30
1000 LJUBLJANA
SLOVENIA
+386 1.519.50.72
EDUARD.CEHOVIN@SIOL.NET
(47)

LIGALUX GMBH
WATERLOOHAIN 5
22769 HAMBURG
GERMANY
+49 40899699299
JM@LIGALUX.DE
(323)

LINA
197 HENRY STREET
SAN FRANCISCO, CA 94114
U.S.A.
415.990.5462
LINA@LINAEDIN.COM
(11, 220, 226)

LLOYD'S GRAPHIC DESIGN LTD.
17 WESTHAVEN PLACE, REDWOODTOWN
BLENHEIM 7301
NEW ZEALAND
+64 3.578.6955
LLOYDGRAPHICS@XTRA.CO.NZ
(143)

LODGE DESIGN CO.
7 S. JOHNSON AVENUE
INDIANAPOLIS, IN 46219
U.S.A.
317.375.4399
EKASS@LODGEDESIGN.COM
(173, 241)

LOEWY
147 GROSVENOR ROAD
LONDON SW1V 3JY
UNITED KINGDOM
+44 20.7798.2098
PAUL.BURGESS@LOEWYGROUP.COM
(18, 35, 36, 46, 72, 90, 94, 102, 122, 125, 276)

LOWERCASE INC.
213 WEST INSTITUTE PLACE, SUITE 311
CHICAGO, IL 60610
U.S.A.
312.274.0652
TIM@LOWERCASEINC.COM
(127, 161)

MAGENTA DESIGN STUDIO
MARJANOVICEV PR. 11
ZAGREB HR 10 000
CROATIA
+385 91.348.2222
DIVA_PAVLICA@INET.HR
(14, 248)

TAMAR MANY AND YANEK IONTEF
SEE: YANEK IONTEF

MAYHEM MEDIA
1939 S. QUEBEC WAY, APT. 407
DENVER, CO 80231
U.S.A.
303.847.9225
ERIC@MAYHEMMEDIA.COM
(38, 75, 374)

ME, ME
19159 E. AURORA DRIVE
WALNUT, CA 91789
U.S.A.
310.801.3606
V@HELLOMEME.COM
(73, 215)

METMARK INTERNATIONAL LTD.
6 KESHET STREET #33
QIRYAT ONO 55401
ISRAEL
+972.3.5371476
(182)

MIRIELLO GRAFICO, INC.
419 WEST G STREET
SAN DIEGO, CA 92101
U.S.A.
619.234.1124
DENNIS@MIRIELLOGRAFICO.COM
(224)

MODERN DOG DESIGN COMPANY
7903 GREENWOOD AVENUE N.
SEATTLE, WA 98103
U.S.A.
206.789.7667
BUBBLES@MODERNDOG.COM
(78, 107)

MORTENSEN DESIGN, INC.
416 BUSH STREET
MOUNTAIN VIEW, CA 94041
U.S.A.
650.988.0946
GORDON@MORTDES.COM
(137, 321, 328, 331, 334)

MUGGIE RAMADANI DESIGN STUDIO
SORTEDAM DOSSERING #55
DK-2100 COPENHAGEN OE
DENMARK
+45 26.70.89.89
CONTACT@MUGGIERAMADANI.COM
(32, 41, 80, 101, 131, 216, 257, 265, 389, 401)

NANCY WU DESIGN
609 WEST 24TH AVENUE
VANCOUVER, BC V5Z 2B7
CANADA
604.327.9891
NIPPY@ULTRANET.CA
(31, 234)

NASSAR DESIGN
11 PARK STREET, SUITE 1
BROOKLINE, MA 09446
U.S.A.
617.264.2862
N.NASSAR@VERIZON.NET
(283, 295)

NB:STUDIO
24 STORE STREET
LONDON WC1E 7BA
UNITED KINGDOM
+44 20.7580.9195
A.DYE@NBSTUDIO.CO.UK
(12, 19, 85, 87, 121, 308, 316, 327, 332)

Ó!
KLAPPARSTÍG 16
REYKJAVÍK 101
ICELAND
+354 562.3300
EINAR@OID.IS
(138)

OCTAVO DESIGN PTY
130 KERR STREET
FITZROY VICTORIA 3065
AUSTRALIA
+61 3.9417.6022
INFO@OCTAVODESIGN.COM.AU
(1, 148, 150, 298, 375)

OTHERWISE INCORPORATED
1144 WEST RANDOLPH STREET
CHICAGO, IL 60607
U.S.A.
312.226.1144
KMIASO@OTHERWISEINC.COM
(71)

OXYGEN DESIGN + COMMUNICATIONS
401 RICHMOND STREET W, SUITE 430
TORONTO, ON M5V 3A8
CANADA
416.506.0202 EXT. 27
ALEX@OXYGEN.CA
(27, 126, 292, 392)

P2DESIGN
3–52 DE LA FALAISE
GATINEAU, QC J8Z 3N9
CANADA
819.790.9277
PASCALE@P2DESIGN.COM
(337)

NIKET PAREKH
306, EVENING STAR, RAHEJA VIHAR
SAKINAKA, OPP. CHANDIVALI STUDIO
ANDHERI (E) MUMBAI 400072
INDIA
+91 98.20930525
NIKETMP@HOTMAIL.COM
(86)

PBS
1320 BRADDOCK PLACE
ALEXANDRIA, VA 22314
U.S.A.
703.739.5006
AZANGARA@PBS.ORG
(114)

PENGUINCUBE
P.O. BOX 113-6117
HAMRA 1103 2100, BEIRUT
LEBANON
+961 3.927380
HOSNI@PENGUINCUBE.COM
(335)

PENSARÉ DESIGN GROUP
729 15TH STREET NW #200
WASHINGTON, DC 20005
U.S.A.
202.638.7700 EXT. 330
MEV@PENSAREDESIGN.COM
(159, 266)

PETERSON + COMPANY
2200 N. LAMAR STREET, SUITE 310
DALLAS, TX 75202
U.S.A.
214.954.0522
MILER@PETERSON.COM
(281)

PH.D
1524A CLOVERFIELD BOULEVARD
SANTA MONICA, CA 90404
U.S.A.
310.829.0900
JOHN@PHDLA.COM
(34, 289, 306, 343, 351)

PHASE05
1163 MAIN STREET
HAMDEN, CT 06514
U.S.A.
203.287.8802
LLOIEWSKI@PHASE05.COM
(163)

PHONOMAT (DIVISION OF EMERGENT PROPERTIES INC.)
FIFTH AVENUE COURT
99 5TH AVENUE, SUITE 249
OTTAWA, ON K1S 5P5
CANADA
613.321.7147
STEFAN@PHONOMAT.CA
(140)

PLAZM
P.O. BOX 2863
PORTLAND, OR 97208
U.S.A.
503.528.8000
JOSH@PLAZM.COM
(56, 170)

BRUNO PORTO
LARGO DOS LEÕES 81 / 905
HUMAITÁ, RIO DE JANEIRO, RJ 22260-210
BRAZIL
+55 21.3472.3699
DESIGN@BRUNOPORTO.COM
(363)

FABRICE PRAEGER
54 BIS RUE DE ERMITAGE
PARIS 75020
FRANCE
+33 1.40.33.17.00
FABRICE.PRAEGER@WANADOO.FR
(200, 287, 366, 398)

PURE
99 MADISON AVENUE, FLOOR 4
NEW YORK, NY 10016
U.S.A.
212.213.2200
TIM@PURENY.COM
(229)

Q
SONNENBERGER STRASSE 16
65193 WIESBADEN
GERMANY
+49 611.181310
INFO@Q-HOME.DE
(7, 93, 197, 255, 403)

R&MAG GRAPHIC DESIGN
VIA DEL PESCATORE 3
8005 CASTELLAMMARE DI STABIA
ITALY
+39 81.8705053
INFO@REMAG.IT
(25, 53, 326, 357)

RAZOR GROOVE GRAPHICS
9951 HIDDEN WAY
GARDEN GROVE, CA 92841
U.S.A.
714.206.0985
ROLANDO@RAZORGROOVE.COM
(315)

REACTOR STUDIO
10811 W. 56TH STREET
SHAWNEE, KS 66203
U.S.A.
913.962.1828
CLIFBO@REACTORSTUDIO.COM
(285)

REDBEAN
582 GROVE STREET #11
SAN FRANCISCO, CA 94102
U.S.A.
415.252.1089
MELISSA@REDBEAN.COM
(213, 247)

RED CANOE
347 CLEAR CREEK TRAIL
DEER LODGE, TN 37726
U.S.A.
423.965.2223
STUDIO@REDCANOE.COM
(250)

RICK JOHNSON & COMPANY
1120 PENNSYLVANIA AVENUE NE
ALBUQUERQUE, NM 87110
U.S.A.
505.266.1100
TMCGRATH@RJC.COM
(365)

DAVID ROJAS
AV. UNIVERSIDAD 1953 / E. 12-602
COPILCO 04340
MEXICO, D.F.
MEXICO
+52 55.2313.7210
DVDRJS@HOTMAIL.COM
(77)

ROMEN DESIGN
BOERGOORN 13
ASSEN 9403 NX
THE NETHERLANDS
+31 592.344006
INFO@ROMENDESIGN.NL
(139)

RULE29
821 KINDBERG COURT
ELBURN, IL 60119
U.S.A.
630.365.5420
JUSTIN@RULE29.COM
(99)

S. M. KINNEY DESIGN
318 KENNEDY STREET
ISELIN, NJ 08830
U.S.A.
732.221.3519
SMKINNEY@COMCAST.NET
(132)

SAMATAMASON
601–289 ALEXANDER STREET
VANCOUVER, BC V6A 4H6
CANADA
604.684.6060
ANN@SAMATAMASON.COM
(89, 284)

SATELLITE DESIGN
539 BRYANT STREET, #305
SAN FRANCISCO, CA 94107
U.S.A.
415.371.1610
AMY@SATELLITE-DESIGN.COM
(10, 360)

SELTZER DESIGN
45 NEWBURY STREET, SUITE 406
BOSTON, MA 02116
U.S.A.
617.353.0303
RS@SELTZERDESIGN.COM
(9)

SEVANS DESIGN
434 E 73RD STREET
KANSAS CITY, MO 64131
U.S.A.
816.237.1060
SEVANSDESIGN@MAC.COM
(386)

SIBLEY PETEET DESIGN – DALLAS
3232 MCKINNEY AVENUE, SUITE 1200
DALLAS, TX 75204
U.S.A.
214.969.1050
BRANDON@SPDDALLAS.COM
(199)

SILVER LINING DESIGN
373 HARVARD STREET, NUMBER 4
BROOKLINE, MA 02446
U.S.A.
617.734.4921
TRISHLEAVITT@COMCAST.NET
(293)

SJI ASSOCIATES
1001 6TH AVENUE, 23RD FLOOR
NEW YORK, NY 10018
U.S.A.
212.391.7770
JILL@SJIASSOCIATES.COM
(3)

SKY DESIGN
50 HURT PLAZA, SUITE 500
ATLANTA, GA 30303
U.S.A.
404.688.4702
SKYDESIGN@AT.ASDNET.COM
(208)

SLANT, INC.
4310 WESTSIDE DRIVE, SUITE F
DALLAS, TX 75209
U.S.A.
214.528.3322
WHATUP@SLANTDESIGN.COM
(95, 176, 341, 369, 370)

SAM SMIDT
666 HIGH STREET
PALO ALTO, CA 94301
U.S.A.
650.327.0707
SAM@SAMSMIDT.COM
(167)

SONSOLES LLORENS, S.L.
CASPE 56, 4º D
08010 BARCELONA
SPAIN
+34 934.124.171
INFO@SONSOLES.COM
(396, 406)

SPACEDUST DESIGN
3516 W. 83RD STREET #111
PRAIRIE VILLAGE, KS 66208
U.S.A.
816.547.9263
SPACEDUSTDESIGN@GMAIL.COM
(158)

SPARKY DESIGN
600 E. 73RD STREET
KANSAS CITY, MO 64131
U.S.A.
816.523.0641
SARAH@SPARKYDESIGN.COM
(98)

SPLASH INTERACTIVE
1103–33 BLOOR ST. EAST
TORONTO, ON M4W 3H1
CANADA
416.928.0465
IVY@SPLASHINTERACTIVE.COM
(190, 372)

STAZER DESIGN
LIBORISTRASSE 35
44143 DORTMUND
GERMANY
+49 231.9598.495
INFO@STAZERDESIGN.DE
(280, 329)

STEERSMCGILLAN LTD.
6–8 COTTERELL COURT, MONMOUTH PLACE
BATH BA1 2NP
UNITED KINGDOM
+44 1225.465546
INFO@STEERSMCGILLAN.CO.UK
(37, 113)

STILRADAR
SCHWABSTRASSE 10A
70197 STUTTGART
GERMANY
+49 711.887.55.20
INFO@STILRADAR.DE
(76, 115, 152, 33, 350)

STOECKER DESIGN
740 16TH AVENUE
MENLO PARK, CA 94025
U.S.A.
650.868.8114
JSTOECKER@MEGAPATHDSL.NET
(336)

STYLOROUGE
57–60 CHARLOTTE ROAD
LONDON EC2A 3QT
UNITED KINGDOM
+44 20.7729.1005
JAMIE@STYLOROUGE.CO.UK
(60)

SUBSTANCE151
2304 E. BALTIMORE STREET
BALTIMORE, MD 21224
U.S.A.
410.732.8379
IDA.CHEINMAN@SUBSTANCE151.COM
(302, 349)

SUM DESIGN
THE SHELDON BUILDING
1 BALTIC PLACE
LONDON N1 5AQ
UNITED KINGDOM
+44 20.7524.5035
LORINDA@SUMDESIGN.CO.UK
(210)

TAXI STUDIO
93 PRINCESS VICTORIA STREET
CLIFTON, BRISTOL
UNITED KINGDOM
+44 117.9735151
KARL@TAXISTUDIO.CO.UK
(129)

TRIANA THE
167 MULBERRY STREET, APT. 5
NEW YORK, NY 10013
U.S.A.
917.573.2684
TRIANATHE@NETSCAPE.NET
(185, 193, 209)

MICHAEL THIELE
ERNST-BECKER-STRASSE 11
44534 LÜNEN
GERMANY
+49 2306.781815
(160)

THINK… BRAND STRATEGY
7 TILNEY COURT, CLERKENWELL
LONDON EC1V 9BQ
UNITED KINGDOM
+44 7958.599737
ED@THINKBRANDSTRATEGY.COM
(379)

THNK GROUP
BLVD. VOJVODE MISICA
BELGRADE, SERBIA 11000
SERBIA & MONTENEGRO
+381 11.3063.900
PREDRAG.MATOVIC@SINTEH.COM
(251)

THOMPSON
THE OLD STABLES, SPRINGWOOD GARDENS
LEEDS, WEST YORKSHIRE LS8 2QB
UNITED KINGDOM
+44 113.232.9222
DAVIDT@THOMPSONDESIGN.CO.UK
(112, 118, 144, 146, 286, 362, 384)

TONIC DESIGN LTD.
4TH FLOOR, 141–143 SHOREDITCH HIGH STREET
LONDON E1 6JE
UNITED KINGDOM
+44 20.7033.2888
EMMA@TONIC.CO.UK
(29, 264)

TRANSMUTE
52 HARDY'S ROAD
CLEETHORPES, N.E. LINCOLNSHIRE
UNITED KINGDOM
+44 01472.699230
CHRIS@TRANSMUTED.CO.UK
(120, 145)

TROLLBÄCK + COMPANY
302 5TH AVENUE, 14TH FLOOR
NEW YORK, NY 10001
U.S.A.
212.529.1010
DEREKH@TROLLBACK.COM
(267)

UNREAL
12 DYOTT STREET
LONDON WC1A 1DE
UNITED KINGDOM
+44 20.7379.8752
BRIAN@UNREAL.CO.UK
(33, 157, 166, 177, 222, 236, 311)

UP DESIGN BUREAU
209 EAST WILLIAM, SUITE 1100
WICHITA, KS 67202
U.S.A.
316.267.1546
CP@UPDESIGNBUREAU.COM
(61–65, 67, 68, 243)

URETSKY + CO.
75 BLEECKER ST. #4A
NEW YORK, NY 10012
U.S.A.
212.777.6259
JAN@URETSKY.NET
(52)

VISUELLE KOMMUNIKATION
BIRSTEINER STRASSE 29
60386 FRANKFURST AM MAIN
GERMANY
+49 69.49.93.41
HH@VK-FFM.DE
(55)

VO6
RUA JOSEPH
BLOCA 49 / 211B2
COPACABANA, RJ 22031-040
BRAZIL
+55 21.2549.4556
YO@YVO6.COM.BR
(164, 361, 409)

WASTE
STUDIO B3.04
31 RUTLAND STREET
LEICESTER
UNITED KINGDOM
+44 116.2616810
INFO@WASTEYOURSELF.COM
(79)

WERBE- & MEDIEN-AKADEMIE MARQUARDT
BORNSTRASSE 241–243
44145 DORTMUND
GERMANY
(26, 51, 119, 181, 187, 191, 194)

WES ANSON DESIGN
2 CHESTERFIELD COURT, GRANVILLE PARK
LONDON
UNITED KINGDOM
+44 7966.500
WES_ANSON@HOTMAIL.COM
(82)

WESTCARR DESIGN
1224 QUINCY STREET #220
MINNEAPOLIS, MN 55413
612-331-4350
DAN@WESTCARR.COM
(169, 304)

WING CHAN DESIGN
167 PERRY STREET, SUITE 5C
NEW YORK, NY 10014
U.S.A.
212.727.9109
WING@WINGCHANDESIGN.COM
(188)

WOLKEN COMMUNICA
2562 DEXTER AVENUE N.
SEATTLE, WA 98109
U.S.A.
206.545.1696
KURT@WOLKENCOMMUNICA.COM
(172, 319, 383, 394, 397)

MARK WOOD
44A CHAUCER ROAD
LONDON SE24 0NU
UNITED KINGDOM
+44 7748.966810
MAIL@MARK-WOOD.NET
(275)

WOW BRANDING
101–1300 RICHARDS STREET
VANCOUVER, BC V6B 3G6
CANADA
866-877-4034
BEMEMORABLE@WOWBRANDING.COM
(96, 123)

ZEIGLER/DACUS
107 EAST CARY STREET
RICHMOND, VA 23219
U.S.A.
804.780.1132
BEND@ZEIGLERDACUS.COM
(252)

ZENDEN
1011 ONTARIO
E. MONTREAL, QC H2L 1P8
CANADA
514.525.7936
INFO@ZENDEN.CC
(108)

ZEROART STUDIO
P.O. BOX 71466
KOWLOON CENTRAL POST OFFICE
HONG KONG
+852 2609.4060
JOLO@ZEROARTSTUDIO.COM
(230)

ZION GRAPHICS
BELLMANSGATAN 8
SE-118 20 STOCKHOLM
SWEDEN
+46 8.644.37.58
RICKY@ZIONGRAPHICS.COM
(6, 39, 124)

ZIP DESIGN LTD.
UNIT 2A
QUEENS STUDIOS
121 SALUSBURY ROAD
LONDON NW6 6RG
UNITED KINGDOM
+44 20.7372.4474
INFO@ZIPDESIGN.CO.UK
(23, 84, 109, 238, 339)

ABOUT THE
AUTHOR

THRYN
RLE

BERG
BOOKS

150 COWLEY ROAD
OXFORD
OX4 1JJ

BERG

01865 254104

WWW.BERGPUBLISHERS.CO.UK
KEARLE@BERGPUBLISHERS.CO.UK

→

LOEWY GROUP IS A FULL SERVICE BRAND COMMUNICATIONS AGENCY. BASED IN LONDON, LOEWY IS AN EXPERT IN THE FIELDS OF BRAND AND IDENTITY DEVELOPMENT. THE AGENCY'S EXPERIENCE SPANS A WIDE RANGE OF SECTORS, WITH OTHER SERVICES INCLUDING ADVERTISING, DIRECT MARKETING, CORPORATE COMMUNICATIONS, PACKAGING, AND NEW MEDIA. EXPERIENCED IN BOTH THE B2C AND B2B MARKETS, LOEWY'S WORK CONTINUES TO REFLECT THE LEGACY OF ITS LEGENDARY FOUNDER, RAYMOND LOEWY.

OTHER ROCKPORT TITLES PRODUCED IN ASSOCIATION WITH LOEWY INCLUDE 1000 GRAPHIC ELEMENTS, BEST OF BROCHURE DESIGN 7, AND 1000 TYPE TREATMENTS.

WWW.LOEWYGROUP.COM